STUDENT UNIT GUIDE

NEW EDITION

AQA AS Law Unit 2
The Concept of Liability

Peter Darwent and Ian Yule

Philip Allan, an imprint of Hodder Education, an Hachette UK company, Market Place, Deddington, Oxfordshire OX15 0SE

Orders
Bookpoint Ltd, 130 Milton Park, Abingdon, Oxfordshire OX14 4SB
tel: 01235 827827
fax: 01235 400401
e-mail: education@bookpoint.co.uk
Lines are open 9.00 a.m.–5.00 p.m., Monday to Saturday, with a 24-hour message answering service. You can also order through the Philip Allan website: www.philipallan.co.uk

© Peter Darwent and Ian Yule 2012

ISBN 978-1-4441-7157-0

First printed 2012
Impression number 5 4 3 2 1
Year 2016 2015 2014 2013 2012

Cover photo: blas/Fotolia

Typeset by Integra Software Services Pvt. Ltd., Pondicherry, India

Printed in Dubai

Hachette UK's policy is to use papers that are natural, renewable and recyclable products and made from wood grown in sustainable forests. The logging and manufacturing processes are expected to conform to the environmental regulations of the country of origin.

P2091

Contents

Getting the most from this book

Examiner tips

Advice from the examiner on key points in the text to help you learn and recall unit content, avoid pitfalls, and polish your exam technique in order to boost your grade.

Knowledge check

Rapid-fire questions throughout the Content Guidance section to check your understanding.

Knowledge check answers

1 Turn to the back of the book for the Knowledge check answers.

Summary

Summaries

- Each core topic is rounded off by a bullet-list summary for quick-check reference of what you need to know.

Questions & Answers

Exam-style questions

Examiner comments on the questions
Tips on what you need to do to gain full marks, indicated by the icon ⓔ.

Sample student answers
Practise the questions, then look at the student answers that follow each set of questions.

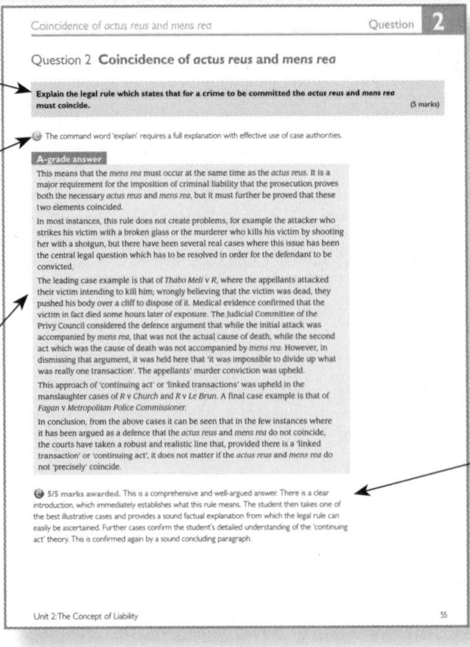

Examiner commentary on sample student answers
Find out how many marks each answer would be awarded in the exam and then read the examiner comments (preceded by the icon ⓔ) following each student answer.

[Sample reproduced exam page, partially legible:]

Coincidence of *actus reus* and *mens rea*   Question **2**

Question 2 **Coincidence of *actus reus* and *mens rea***

Explain the legal rule which states that for a crime to be committed the *actus reus* and *mens rea* must coincide. (5 marks)

ⓔ The command word 'explain' requires a full explanation with effective use of case authorities.

A-grade answer

This means that the *mens rea* must occur at the same time as the *actus reus*. It is a major requirement for the imposition of criminal liability that the prosecution proves both the necessary *actus reus* and *mens rea*, but it must further be proved that these two elements coincided.

In most instances, this rule does not create problems, for example the attacker who strikes his victim with a broken glass or the murderer who kills his victim by shooting her with a shotgun, but there have been several real cases where this issue has been the central legal question which has to be resolved in order for the defendant to be convicted.

The leading case example is that of *Thabo Meli v R*, where the appellants attacked their victim intending to kill him; wrongly believing that the victim was dead, they pushed his body over a cliff to dispose of it. Medical evidence confirmed that the victim in fact died some hours later of exposure. The Judicial Committee of the Privy Council considered the defence argument that while the initial attack was accompanied by *mens rea*, that was not the actual cause of death, while the second act which was the cause of death was not accompanied by *mens rea*. However, in dismissing that argument, it was held here that 'it was impossible to divide up what was really one transaction'. The appellants' murder conviction was upheld.

This approach of 'continuing act' or 'linked transactions' was upheld in the manslaughter cases of *R v Church* and *R v Le Brun*. A final case example is that of *Fagan v Metropolitan Police Commissioner*.

In conclusion, from the above cases it can be seen that in the few instances where it has been argued as a defence that the *actus reus* and *mens rea* do not coincide, the courts have taken a robust and realistic line that, provided there is a 'linked transaction' or 'continuing act', it does not matter if the *actus reus* and *mens rea* do not 'precisely' coincide.

ⓔ 5/5 marks awarded. This is a comprehensive and well-argued answer. There is a clear introduction, which immediately establishes what this rule means. The student then takes one of the best illustrative cases and provides a sound factual explanation from which the legal rule can easily be ascertained. Further cases confirm the student's detailed understanding of the 'continuing act' theory. This is confirmed again by a sound concluding paragraph.

Unit 2: The Concept of Liability   55

About this book

This unit guide is for students following the AQA AS Law course. **Unit 2: The Concept of Liability** makes up the substantive, i.e. 'real law', element for AS. The legal topics covered are those of criminal liability and a choice between the tort law of negligence and contract law.

The examination for this unit is 1 hour 30 minutes. In this time, you must answer two out of three scenario-based questions — a compulsory criminal law question and a further question from either tort or contract law:

- The first scenario will deal with some form of criminal attack. You will be required to answer a general question on an issue relating to criminal liability and then to identify from the scenario which offences may have been committed.
- The second scenario addresses either the tort of negligence or contract law.
- Each scenario question will also test your knowledge of either sentencing (concentrating on the different types of sentence available) or compensatory damages, and of criminal or civil court procedure.

There are two sections to this guide:

- **Content Guidance** — this sets out the specification content for Unit 2. It also contains references to cases that you will need to study in order to achieve a sound understanding of each topic.
- **Questions and Answers** — this provides 11 questions, as well as sample A- and C/D-grade answers. Examiner's comments show how marks are awarded or why they are withheld. As this is a substantive law module, it is particularly important to be able to use case law effectively. The Questions and Answers section gives examples of how to employ case and statutory references to best effect.

Content Guidance

Introduction to criminal liability

Underlying principles of criminal liability

The traditional basis for criminal liability — that is, liability to be prosecuted in a criminal court and, if convicted, to be punished by the state — is an *actus reus* (the physical element) accompanied by the appropriate *mens rea* (the mental element). This section looks at these two important concepts in detail.

It is a general principle of criminal law that a person may not be convicted of a crime unless the prosecution has proved beyond doubt that he or she:

- has caused a certain event, or responsibility is to be attributed to him or her for the existence of a certain state of affairs, which is forbidden by criminal law
- had a defined state of mind (*mens rea*) in relation to the event or state of affairs (*actus reus*)

Actus reus

Actus reus literally means the 'guilty act' and is made up of all the parts of the crime except the defendant's mental state. While most crimes require the accused to commit a certain act, this is not always the case, and criminal liability can also arise through a failure to act (an omission) and from a certain type of conduct. Few crimes can be adequately described simply by reference to the act; most require proof of accompanying circumstances and of a particular consequence. For example, in criminal damage the offence consists of destroying or damaging property that belongs to another (the act) and there being no lawful excuse (the circumstances).

Each separate crime has its own specific *actus reus*. For battery, it is the infliction of unlawful personal violence. For assault occasioning actual bodily harm, it is both the original assault or (more usually) battery and the actual bodily harm suffered by the victim as a consequence.

Note also that while *mens rea* may exist without an *actus reus*, if the *actus reus* of a particular crime does not exist or occur, that crime is not committed.

Ordinarily, the prosecution must prove that the accused person voluntarily brought about the *actus reus* of the crime — that is, the act or omission must have occurred because of a **conscious exercise of will** of the defendant. If in an assault case the defendant's arm was physically forced by another to strike the victim, or if the defendant was pushed against the victim by another person, there would be no crime by the defendant, although it is probable that the perpetrator of the force would be guilty of crimes against both the defendant and the victim. In *Hill* v *Baxter* (1958), the trial judge gave a useful *hypothetical* example: if a swarm of bees flew through an open car window and caused the driver to lose control of the vehicle, he or she would not be liable for a resulting accident. This would be an instance of an involuntary act, so there would be no *actus reus*.

Knowledge check 1

What is meant by the term *'actus reus'*?

Crimes of omission

As well as actions, such as hitting someone over the head or stealing a wallet, an *actus reus* can also be an **omission** or failure to act. In most criminal prosecutions, the prosecutor will be seeking to prove that a prohibited situation or result has been brought about by the acts of the defendant. However, in certain situations the defendant's failure to act will have led to the prohibited event occurring.

Most jurisdictions, including that of England and Wales, have not adopted a general principle of liability for failing to act — a **'Good Samaritan law'**. Instead, the law has defined certain factual situations in which persons are under a duty to act. If they fail to act in these situations, thereby causing a prohibited criminal result, they shall be liable for that result.

There are five areas where such liability for omissions exists:

- **Duty arising from a contract.** This occurs when a failure to perform a contractual obligation endangers life. In *R* v *Pittwood* (1902), a railway crossing gatekeeper opened the gate to let a cart through and went off to lunch, forgetting to shut it again. Ten minutes later a haycart, while crossing the line, was struck by a train and the driver was killed. The gatekeeper was convicted of manslaughter on the ground that 'there was gross and criminal negligence, as the man was paid to keep the gate shut and protect the public... A man may incur criminal liability from a duty arising out of contract'.
- **Duty arising from statute.** An Act of Parliament can make it an offence to fail to act in defined circumstances. For example, under s.1(1) of the **Children and Young Persons Act 1933**, the House of Lords ruled that the *actus reus* of the offence is simply the failure for whatever reason to provide the child with the necessary medical care. Other examples include offences under the **Road Traffic Act 1988**, such as failure to wear a seatbelt or failure to stop and report a road accident.
- **Voluntary assumption of a duty.** If someone voluntarily takes responsibility for another person, he or she also assumes the positive duty to act for the general welfare of that person. In *R* v *Stone and Dobinson* (1977), an unmarried cohabiting couple invited Stone's middle-aged sister, who was anorexic, to live with them. Although Stone and Dobinson were aware that the woman was neglecting herself and that her health was deteriorating rapidly, they did nothing to assist her, such as summoning medical help or informing social services. Three years after she came to live with them, she was found dead in her bed, naked and severely emaciated. The cause of death was toxaemia from infected bed sores and prolonged immobilisation. Stone and Dobinson were convicted of her manslaughter — they had assumed a duty of care for her, a duty that they could easily have discharged by calling for help or by providing even basic care.

- **Duty arising from prior conduct.** If the defendant accidentally commits an act that causes harm, and subsequently becomes aware of the danger he or she has created, there arises a duty to act reasonably to avert that danger. In *R* v *Miller* (1983), Lord Diplock had no doubts that the defendant had been convicted correctly. This was because the *actus reus* of the offence of arson is present if the defendant accidentally starts a fire and fails to take any steps to extinguish it or prevent damage, due to an intention to destroy or damage property belonging to another or being reckless regarding whether any such property would be destroyed or damaged (as in this case). The defendant, by his own admission, became aware of the fire and chose to do nothing. Note that this case is *not* suggesting liability for purely accidental fire. If, when Miller realised he had started a fire, he had tried to phone the fire brigade or had alerted neighbours, he would not have incurred criminal liability, even if in the meantime the fire had spread to an adjoining gas-holder and half the town had blown up.
- **Public duty.** A person in a public office may be under a duty to care for others. In *R* v *Dytham* (1979), a police officer was held to be guilty of a crime when, without justification, he failed to perform his duty to preserve the Queen's Peace by not protecting a citizen who was being kicked to death.

It is essential that you learn statutory and/or case references for each of the above rules — they are one of the key elements that examiners are looking for.

The most common examples of omissions in exam questions are those of 'assumed responsibility', where a relative or other responsible adult takes on responsibility for the care of a child, and the 'dangerous situation', where the defendant has accidentally created a dangerous situation and has thus simultaneously put him- or herself under a duty of care to do something about it.

There are also **circumstance crimes** or **state of affairs offences**, where the *actus reus* is simply that a particular circumstance has occurred, for example the circumstance of being drunk and in control of a motor vehicle. Other such offences are possession crimes, where the defendant is in possession of stolen goods, a firearm or illegal drugs.

Rules of causation

Another issue that needs to be understood is causation. This occurs in so-called **result crimes** — those where the defendant's actions cause the prohibited result. In murder, for example, the prosecution must prove a causal link between the defendant's actions and the death of the victim.

Factual causation

The factual rule of causation, referred to as the **'but for' test**, simply requires the prosecution to prove that 'but for' the defendant's act, the harm would not have occurred. This is well illustrated by the famous case of *R* v *White* (1910), where the defendant put potassium cyanide into a drink with intent to murder his mother. She was found dead shortly afterwards with the glass, three-quarters filled, beside her. The medical evidence showed that she had died not of poisoning, but of heart failure. The defendant was acquitted of murder and convicted of attempted murder. Although

Examiner tip

If a question requires *actus reus* to be explained, ensure that you include omissions as these are based on case examples. Two or three examples of omissions will be enough.

the consequence that the defendant intended had occurred, he did not cause it to occur and therefore there was no *actus reus* of murder.

Legal causation

While it is usually easy to prove the 'but for' rule, there are many situations where the question of causation is much more difficult to establish clearly. A. M. Dugdale in *A Level Law* (Butterworths, 3rd edn, 1996) lists some examples:

- A points a gun at B and B dies of a heart attack.
- A knocks B unconscious and leaves him lying in a road, where he is run over by a car and killed.
- A injures B, who is being taken by ambulance to the hospital. The ambulance crashes, killing all the occupants.
- A knocks B unconscious and she remains lying in a street for several hours, where she is robbed, raped or assaulted further.

In all these examples, it could be argued that A caused the consequences, on the basis that none of these events would have happened 'but for' the initial attack by A on B. The obvious difficulty with this approach, however, is that it can link an initial cause (the attack) with consequences that are both highly improbable and unforeseeable. This has been a particular problem in cases of unlawful killing — murder and manslaughter — where there is a less direct link between act and effect. In such cases, one has to consider the responsibility of the defendant for the victim's death.

At one time, the legal position was that the defendant was liable for all natural and probable consequences of his or her voluntary acts, but this presumption has now been overturned on the grounds that it could link together events that are connected too remotely. In *R v Marjoram* (1999), the trial judge instructed the jury to consider the legal cause — there must be something that could reasonably be foreseen as a consequence of the unlawful act. Nowadays, it is accepted law that the defendant need only have made 'a significant contribution' to the unlawful result, as in *R v Cheshire* (1991), or have been an 'operative and substantial cause of harm'.

Another case exemplifying this principle is *R v Smith* (1959). The defendant was involved in a fight with a fellow soldier, during which he stabbed the victim twice with a bayonet. The victim was taken to the medical centre but was dropped twice during the journey. The medical officer did not notice the victim had been stabbed in the back, causing lung damage, and gave treatment that was later described as 'thoroughly bad'. The victim died and the defendant argued that he was not responsible for his death because the chain of causation had been broken by the way in which the victim had been treated. However, the defendant was convicted of murder because the stab wound was the 'operating and substantial cause' of death:

> If at the time of death the original wound is still the operating and substantial cause, then the death can properly be said to be the result of the wound, albeit some other cause of death is also operating. Only if it can be said that the original wound is merely the setting in which another cause operates can it be said that the death does not result from the wound.

Examiner tip

In a causation question, you are required to explain the factual rule briefly, but be sure to describe the facts in *White* accurately.

Knowledge check 2

Why was Jordan's conviction for manslaughter quashed?

The latter situation occurred in the case of *R v Jordan* (1956), where the victim of a serious injury made a good recovery in hospital, but while recuperating received an injection of a drug to which he was allergic. The doctors confirmed that the death was caused not by the original wound, which was mainly healed at the time of death, but by the injection (and also the intravenous introduction of large quantities of liquid).

Further rules that occur in causation address the question of what constitutes a new intervening act (*novus actus interveniens*). This requires something that cannot be foreseen, and it must be so overwhelming as to invalidate the original *actus reus*. For example, consider a situation where A shoots at B and causes B serious internal injuries, which could be treated successfully if immediate and specialised medical treatment were provided. However, the ambulance takes 10 minutes to arrive and as a result B dies. This is a foreseeable result and A is guilty of murder. **'Acts of God'**, however, such as earthquakes and tidal waves, are regarded as intervening acts and will therefore break the causal chain. Note also what are called **escape cases**, in which the victim has suffered injury or has been killed while trying to escape from a serious attack. In such cases, the defendant will be liable if the victim's conduct in running away was within the range of foreseeable responses to the defendant's behaviour. This occurred in *R v Roberts* (1971) (see p. 18).

The 'thin skull' rule

The 'thin skull' rule dictates that if some pre-existing weakness or medical condition of the victim makes the result of an attack more severe than it would be ordinarily, the defendant cannot argue that the chain of causation has been broken. It is also known as 'you take your victims as you find them'. For example, if the victim has an abnormally thin skull, a blow on the head could cause serious injury or even death, whereas in a 'normal' person it would usually only cause a bruise. The attacker would be liable for the more serious injury or the death.

Examiner tip

In a general 'explain the rules of causation' question, in addition to factual causation, be sure to explain — with relevant cases — medical negligence, 'escape' and 'thin skull' rules.

This rule covers not only physical but also mental conditions, and even the victim's beliefs or values, as in *R v Blaue* (1975). Here, the victim of a stabbing was a Jehovah's Witness, who refused on religious grounds to accept a blood transfusion that would have saved her life. The defendant was convicted of her manslaughter and the Court of Appeal rejected his appeal, holding that the victim's refusal to accept the transfusion did not break the causal chain.

In most of the questions that are likely to be asked in this unit, this issue should not present too many difficulties, but remember that these rules are even more important if you study fatal offences in Unit 3.

Mens rea

Having looked at issues of *actus reus* — the physical element in a crime — we now need to examine the even more important areas dealt with under *mens rea* — the mental element necessary for all serious crimes. Criminal law does not exist to punish a person who has simply committed some kind of wrongful action; to be criminally liable, that person must have carried out the wrongful act in circumstances in which blame can be attached to his or her conduct. To put it more simply, a criminal is punished not so much on account of what he or she has done, but because of *why* he or she did it. All the crimes that form part of Unit 2 — non-fatal offences — and those that are included in later A2 units have both a separate *actus reus* and *mens rea*. The following states of mind are used to denote *mens rea*:

- **intention** — where the offender makes a decision to break the law
- **recklessness** — where the offender acts while realising that there is a possibility that his or her action could cause the illegal outcome
- **gross negligence** — where the defendant did not foresee causing any harm, but should have realised the risks involved. An example is *R* v *Adomako* (1995), where an anaesthetist failed to notice for 6 minutes that an oxygen tube had become disconnected from the ventilator. By this time, the patient had suffered a cardiac arrest and attempts to resuscitate were unsuccessful.

For the crimes studied in Unit 2, it is enough that you understand the issues surrounding intention and recklessness. All non-fatal offences — except s.18 wounding or causing grievous bodily harm with intent — can be committed either intentionally or recklessly.

Intention

The meaning of intention is not found in any statute but in judicial decisions. It is clear that a person intends a result when it is his or her aim, objective or purpose to bring it about. This might be termed **'dictionary intention'**. In *R* v *Mohan* (1976) the Court of Appeal defined intent as 'a decision to bring about the commission of an offence, no matter whether the defendant desired that consequence of his act or not.'

However, the concept of intention is subject to ambiguity. What is the position when someone has clearly caused an illegal result, realising that it would almost certainly occur, although it was not his or her primary intention? There is a well-known hypothetical example of a person placing a bomb in an aircraft, with the intention that it will explode when the plane reaches an altitude of 20,000 feet. His specific aim or objective is to obtain the insurance money on the lost aircraft. In these circumstances, he surely knows that when the plane explodes all the passengers and crew will be killed, but does he really intend their deaths? This type of case is one of **oblique intention**.

In *R* v *Hancock and Shankland* (1986), this issue was at the heart of the case — how the law should deal with a defendant who has created an unlawful result where it is clear that the outcome was probable and the defendant may well have foreseen it.

The defendants were Welsh coal miners on strike, and when one of their fellow miners wanted to return to work, they tried to stop him. The 'strike-breaker' was driven in a taxi to another coal mine, and the route was via a motorway. The defendants knew that the taxi would pass under a particular bridge and when the taxi drove under it they pushed concrete blocks onto the road below. One of the blocks hit the windscreen of the taxi and the driver was killed. The defendants claimed that their only intention was to block the road and prevent the strike-breaker from reaching the coal mine, not to kill the driver of the taxi. Had they been charged with manslaughter, they would have pleaded guilty; however, the charge was murder, which requires intention to kill or commit serious injury.

> **Examiner tip**
> You need to be aware that oblique intent is only relevant for offences of specific intent, i.e. for s.18 causing grievous bodily harm with intent. Do *not* refer to oblique intent for any other offence.

Although the defendants were convicted of murder at their trial, the Court of Appeal and the House of Lords both quashed that conviction and substituted a manslaughter conviction, holding that the issue of intention had not been established.

Lord Scarman indicated that, in cases like these, juries needed to be told by the judge that 'the greater the probability of a consequence occurring, the more likely it was so foreseen and, if so, the more likely it was intended'. This emphasised the point that foresight of the degree of probability was the only evidence from which intention could be inferred.

In the more recent cases of *R* v *Nedrick* (1986) and *R* v *Woollin* (1998) (see below), a tighter rule was laid down for such cases of oblique intent. This now requires juries to return a verdict of murder only where they find that 'the defendant foresaw death or serious injury as a virtually certain consequence of his or her voluntary actions'. It is worth pointing out that, in both these cases, the original murder conviction was changed on appeal to a manslaughter conviction.

R v *Woollin* (1998) resulted from the death of a 3-month-old baby. Although initially the defendant gave a number of different explanations, he finally admitted that he had 'lost his cool' when his baby started to choke. He had shaken the baby and then, in a fit of rage or frustration, had thrown him in the direction of his pram, which was standing against the wall some 3 or 4 feet away. He knew that the baby's head had hit something hard but denied intending to throw him against the wall or wanting him to die or to suffer serious injury. The trial judge did not direct the jury to deal with the issue of intention on the basis of the Nedrick 'foresight of virtually certain consequences' rule and the defendant was convicted of murder.

Knowledge check 3

What rule was laid down in *Nedrick* and *Woollin* about oblique intent?

The Court of Appeal, although critical of the trial judge, dismissed the appeal, and certified questions for the House of Lords. The House of Lords quashed the defendant's conviction for murder and substituted a conviction for manslaughter. Lord Steyn gave the main speech, saying that 'a result foreseen as virtually certain is an intended result'.

In *R* v *Matthews and Alleyne* (2003), the defendants had robbed a student and then, knowing that he could not swim, thrown him into the Thames where he drowned. It was held, confirming their murder conviction, that the 'virtual certainty' rule was evidential, not substantive, but that in practice there was very little difference between a rule of evidence and a rule of substantive law.

Recklessness

A standard dictionary definition of recklessness is 'unjustified risk-taking'. Following the case of *R* v *G and Others* (2003), English law now only recognises subjective ('Cunningham') recklessness.

Cunningham recklessness

The prosecution must prove that the defendant appreciated that his or her action created an unjustified risk and then went ahead with the action anyway. In *R* v *Cunningham* (1957), the defendant ripped a gas meter from a wall to steal the money it contained, causing gas to escape. The gas seeped into a neighbouring building, where it partially asphyxiated a woman. Cunningham was convicted of a s.23 offence — administering a noxious substance — but he appealed successfully on the ground that the prosecution had failed to prove that he recognised the risk of the gas escape. The question was simply whether the defendant *had* foreseen that his act might injure someone, not whether he *ought* to have foreseen this risk.

Coincidence of *actus reus* and *mens rea*

In order for an offence to be committed, the *mens rea* must coincide in point of time with the *actus reus*. If I happen to kill my neighbour accidentally, I do not become a murderer by thereafter expressing joy over his death, even if a week previously I had planned to kill him but had then changed my mind. *Mens rea* implies an intention to carry out a present act, not a future one. In most cases, there is no problem in proving the necessary coincidence of *actus reus* and *mens rea*, but there are a few occasions that illustrate the fact that judges can take a more generous view of this issue of coincidence.

One such case is that of *Thabo Meli* v *R* (1954), where the defendants clearly intended to kill their victim. Having attacked him, they threw what they believed to be his dead body over a cliff in order to dispose of it. The victim in fact survived both the murderous attack and the fall, but died subsequently of exposure. On appeal, the Privy Council ruled that it was 'impossible to divide up what was really one series of acts' and that if during that series of acts the necessary *mens rea* was present, that was sufficient coincidence to justify a conviction. This ruling was followed in *R* v *Church* (1966). A more recent case was *R* v *Le Brun* (1992), where again the view was upheld that where there is a series of actions that can be regarded as a linked transaction or continuing act, the coincidence rule is satisfied, provided that at some point during the transaction the required *mens rea* is present.

A final example is that of *Fagan* v *Metropolitan Police Commissioner* (1969). The defendant had accidentally driven his car onto a police officer's foot when he had been instructed to park his car close to the kerb. When the officer ordered him to move the vehicle, Fagan swore and turned off the ignition. He was later convicted of assaulting a police officer in the execution of his duty. Fagan appealed on the ground that when he drove accidentally onto the officer's foot there was no *mens rea*, and when he had *mens rea* (when he swore and turned off the ignition) there was no act but an omission (failure to act), and the *actus reus* of this particular crime required an act. The appeal was dismissed — the court held that Fagan's driving onto the officer's foot and staying there was one single continuous act rather than an act followed by an omission. So long as the defendant had the *mens rea* at some point during that continuous act, he was liable.

Transferred malice

Under the rule of transferred malice, if A fires a gun at B, intending to kill B, but misses and in fact kills C, A is guilty of murdering C. The intention (malice) is transferred from B to C. This means that the intended victim and the actual victim are treated as if they were the same. The leading case is that of *R* v *Latimer* (1886). In this case, the defendant had a quarrel in a public house with another person. He took off his belt and aimed a blow at his intended victim, which struck him lightly. However, the belt then struck a person standing beside the intended victim and wounded her severely.

Examiner tip

Many students fail to explain the facts of *Cunningham* correctly. Another common error occurs when students answering a problem-solving question merely 'assert' that the defendant *would* have or *should* have recognised he was taking an unjustified risk, instead of considering whether he did.

Knowledge check 4

What rule was decided in *Thabo Meli*?

The jury found that the blow was unlawfully aimed at the original victim but that the striking of the second victim was purely accidental. It was held on appeal, however, that the defendant should be convicted of unlawfully and maliciously wounding the second victim.

The other important aspect of this rule is that it is limited to situations where the *actus reus* and the *mens rea* of the same crime coincide. If A fires a gun at B, intending to kill B, but misses and the bullet breaks a valuable Ming vase, the *mens rea* of damage to property was not present so the intent does not transfer. In *R* v *Pembliton* (1874), the defendant committed the *actus reus* of malicious damage but with the *mens rea* of assault — because of this, he was not guilty of either crime.

Examiner tip

In an explanatory question on transferred malice, include *R* v *Pembliton* to obtain a 'sound' answer.

Strict liability offences

Strict liability offences do not require *mens rea* to be proved. They are often referred to as **'no fault' offences**, and almost all of them are created by statute law. Many of them concern road traffic offences or breaches of health and safety legislation. A good example of such a crime occurred in *Callow* v *Tillstone* (1900), where the defendant, who was a butcher, asked a vet to examine a carcass to ensure it was fit for human consumption. On receiving the vet's assurance that it was fit, the butcher offered it for sale. However, the vet had been negligent and the meat was contaminated. The defendant was convicted of exposing unsound meat for sale, even though he had exercised due care. Another illustrative case is *Harrow LBC* v *Shah* (1999) in which a shopkeeper was convicted of the offence of selling a lottery ticket to a minor child, even though he thought, reasonably, that the boy was at least 16 years old.

The argument most frequently advanced by the courts for imposing strict liability is that it is necessary to do so in the interests of the public. It may be conceded that, in many of the instances where strict liability has been imposed, the public does need protection against negligence in cases involving road safety, workplace safety, food safety and consumer protection.

Assuming that the threat of punishment can make the potential harm-doer more careful, there may be a valid ground for imposing liability for negligence as well as where there is *mens rea*. This is particularly true when the offence involves a non-human consequence such as causing pollution; the courts have consistently ruled that such an offence is one of strict liability. A good illustrative case is *Alphacell* v *Woodward* (1972), where the House of Lords held that the offence of causing polluted matter to enter a river was a strict liability offence.

It is also argued that the majority of strict liability cases can be described as 'administrative' or **'quasi' crimes** — offences that are not criminal 'in any real sense' and are merely acts prohibited in the public interest. Parliament makes no such distinction: an act either is, or is not, declared by Parliament to be a crime, but the courts decide whether it is a 'real' or 'quasi' crime on the basis that an offence which, in the public eye, carries little or no stigma and does not involve 'the disgrace of criminality' is only a 'quasi' crime. In this instance, strict liability may be imposed, because 'it does not offend the ordinary man's sense of justice that moral guilt is not of the essence of the offence'.

This distinction was made in *Sweet* v *Parsley* (1970). Here, Lord Reid acknowledged that strict liability was appropriate for regulatory offences. However, he stated that the kind of crime to which a real social stigma is attached should usually require proof of *mens rea*. In this case, the defendant's conviction for being concerned in the management of premises that were being used for the purpose of smoking cannabis was quashed on appeal, on the ground that such an offence was not one of strict liability and required *mens rea* to be proved. A similar ruling was made in *B* v *DPP* (2006).

In most of these cases, the penalty imposed is a fine and not a community or custodial sentence. However, in *Gammon* v *Attorney-General of Hong Kong* (1985), the Privy Council admitted that the fact that the offence was punishable with a fine of $250,000 and 3 years' imprisonment was not inconsistent with the imposition of strict liability.

Another justification for strict liability offences is that they are much easier and cheaper to prosecute. Many motoring offences — parking and speeding, or using a mobile phone while driving — usually result in a fixed fine penalty rather than a prosecution before magistrates.

Knowledge check 5

Why did the House of Lords decide that Mrs Sweet was not guilty?

Non-fatal offences

Now that you have studied the theory in terms of *actus reus* and *mens rea*, you can apply it to actual offences — those grouped together as non-fatal offences (Table 1). There are five of these:

- assault
- battery
- assault occasioning actual bodily harm (ABH)
- malicious wounding or inflicting grievous bodily harm (GBH)
- wounding or causing grievous bodily harm with intent (to cause GBH)

Table 1 Summary of non-fatal offences

Crime	Actus reus	Mens rea	Cases
Assault	Causing the victim to apprehend immediate, unlawful personal violence	Intention or subjective recklessness to causing *actus reus*	*Logdon, Ireland, Constanza, Venna*
Battery	Infliction of unlawful personal violence	Intention or subjective recklessness as to inflicting unlawful personal violence	*Fagan, Thomas, Haystead*
Section 47 ABH	Assault or battery causing actual bodily harm	Intention or recklessness as to the assault or battery	*Miller, Chan-Fook, Savage, Parmenter, Roberts*
Section 20 GBH/ wounding	Wounding: all layers of skin must be broken; GBH: serious injury	Intention or recklessness as to *some* harm	*Eisenhower, Smith, Mowatt, Grimshaw*
Section 18 GBH with intent	Wounding or GBH as in s.20	Specific intent to cause GBH, or intent to resist lawful arrest	*Nedrick, Woollin*

Assault and battery were two distinct crimes at common law and their separate existence is confirmed by s.39 of the **Criminal Justice Act 1988**. The other three more serious offences are defined in the **Offences Against the Person Act 1861**.

Assault

This is any act by which the defendant, intentionally or recklessly, causes the victim to apprehend immediate and unlawful personal violence. In other words, this offence can be described as 'a threat of violence which the victim believes to be a threat'.

Accordingly, if any harm is caused, a more serious offence than assault has been committed, although the defendant may also have committed an assault. An example would be if the defendant shouted at the victim 'I am going to thump you' and then proceeded to do just that.

Actus reus *of assault*

In a typical case of assault (as opposed to battery), the defendant, by some physical movement, causes the victim to believe that he or she is about to be struck. There may even be an assault where the defendant has no intention of committing battery or has no means of carrying out the threat.

Examiner tip

You need to get this definition correct — the victim only has to believe that he/she may be about to be attacked.

The issues to be decided are whether the defendant intends to cause the victim to believe that he or she can and will carry it out, and whether the victim does believe this. It is clear that a threat to inflict harm at some future time cannot amount to an assault — an apprehension of *immediate* personal violence is essential.

However, there is a tendency to enlarge the concept of assault by taking a generous view of 'immediacy', to include threats in which the impending impact is more remote. In *Logdon* v *DPP* (1976), it was held that the defendant committed an assault by showing his victim a pistol in a drawer and declaring that he would hold her hostage. In *Smith* v *Superintendent of Woking Police* (1983), the defendant committed an assault by looking at the victim in her nightclothes through a window, intending to frighten her.

It was made clear in *R* v *Ireland* (1998) that an assault may be committed by words alone, or even, as in that case, by silent telephone calls where the caller 'intends by his silence to cause fear and he is so understood'.

Knowledge check 6

What ruling concerning 'immediacy' was made in *Smith* v *Supt. of Woking Police*?

In *R* v *Constanza* (1997), it was held that there had been an assault when the victim read the letters that had been sent by a stalker and interpreted them as clear threats — there was a 'fear of violence at some time not excluding the immediate future'.

Mens rea *of assault*

This can be either intention or subjective recklessness as to causing the victim to apprehend immediate unlawful personal violence — *R* v *Venna* (1976).

Battery

This is defined as 'any act by which the defendant, intentionally or recklessly, inflicts unlawful personal violence'. Most batteries involve an assault, although this is not a requirement — a blow to the back of the head, completely taking the victim by surprise, is a battery. Examples of battery include a push, a kiss, and throwing a projectile or water that lands on another's body.

While it used to be accepted that battery does not need to be hostile or aggressive, in *Wilson* v *Pringle* (1987), Croom-Johnson LJ stated that a touching had to be hostile to amount to battery, and in Brown and Others (1993), the House of Lords approved that ruling when Lord Jauncey described hostility as 'a necessary ingredient'.

Many unwanted touchings are 'technical' batteries, and prosecutors are relied upon to avoid prosecutions of minor incidents. Since the merest touching without consent is a criminal offence, the demands of everyday life require that there is an implied consent to that degree of contact which is necessary or customary in ordinary life. Therefore, no one can complain of the jostling inevitable in a supermarket, for example.

Actus reus *of battery*

This consists of the infliction of unlawful personal violence by the defendant. The use of the term 'violence' here is misleading — all that is required for a battery is that the defendant touches the victim without consent or other lawful excuse.

There may also be a battery when the defendant inadvertently applies force to the victim and then wrongfully refuses to withdraw it (*Fagan* v *Metropolitan Police Commissioner*, 1969). It is also settled law that there can be a battery where there has been no direct contact with the victim's body — touching his or her clothing may be enough to constitute this offence. In *R* v *Thomas* (1985), it was stated that touching the woman's skirt was equivalent to touching the woman herself.

Battery may be inflicted indirectly as in *Haystead* v *Chief Constable of Derbyshire* (2000) where the defendant twice punched a woman who was holding her baby, which caused her to drop the baby who was then injured. The defendant was convicted of battering the baby.

Mens rea *of battery*

The law is settled that either intention or recklessness as to the infliction of unlawful personal violence is sufficient. After a brief period of uncertainty, it is now clear that subjective recklessness — 'the conscious taking of an unjustified risk' — is the relevant test (confirmed by the cases of *R* v *Venna*, 1976 and *R* v *Savage*; *R* v *Parmenter*, 1991). The defendant must foresee the risk of causing the application of violence.

Assault occasioning actual bodily harm (s.47)

Here the word 'assault' can mean either assault *or* battery, but most often it will refer to battery — the infliction of some unlawful violence rather than a threat of violence.

Examiner tip

Note that the *actus reus* for this offence requires there to have been either an assault or (more usually) a battery which has caused ABH. Therefore, in a problem-solving question dealing with s.47 ABH, you must explain both the *actus reus* and *mens rea* of the initial offence, before continuing to explain actual bodily harm.

Examiner tip

Make sure you understand this *mens rea* rule — failure to do so is one of the most common causes of mistakes made by students in exams.

Knowledge check 7

What definition of actual bodily harm was laid down in *R v Miller*?

This offence is triable either way and carries a maximum sentence of 5 years' imprisonment. The conduct element (*actus reus*) is an assault or battery that causes 'actual bodily harm' (ABH). This has been given the wide definition of 'any hurt or injury calculated to interfere with the health or comfort of the victim', provided it is not 'merely transient or trifling' (see *R v Miller*, 1954). In *R v Chan-Fook* (1994), the Court of Appeal stated that the injury 'should not be so trivial as to be wholly insignificant'. In *R v Smith* (2007), it was held by the Court of Appeal that the defendant cutting his girlfriend's hair was sufficient to constitute ABH.

One consequence of this definition is that it has been held to cover psychological harm — where the defendant causes the victim to become hysterical or to suffer substantial fear (see *R v Chan-Fook*, 1994). Note, however, that in *R v Morris* (1998) the Court of Appeal held that evidence from the victim's doctor that she suffered from anxiety, fear, tearfulness, sleeplessness and physical tension was insufficient to establish ABH.

The *mens rea* required for ABH is the same as for battery — intention or recklessness as to the application of some unlawful force to another. This important rule was established in the separate cases of *Savage* and *Parmenter*, where it was held by the House of Lords that the prosecution is not obliged for a s.47 offence to prove that the defendant intended to cause some actual bodily harm or was reckless as to whether such harm would be caused.

In *R v Savage* (1991), the defendant admitted throwing the contents of her beer glass over the victim during a bar brawl. The glass slipped out of her hand and broke, and a piece of glass cut the victim's wrist. Although the defendant denied intending to cause the injury suffered by the victim, intending only to throw the beer over her, she was convicted of s.47 ABH. This means that a guilty verdict may be returned upon proof of an assault, together with proof of the fact that actual bodily harm was occasioned by the assault. This is a key legal point that examiners are looking for — and one of the most common mistakes made in examination answers. Few marks are awarded for mentioning the *mens rea* of s.47 ABH as intention or recklessness, unless there is a clear reference to this issue and these cases.

R v Roberts (1971) confirms that the *mens rea* of s.47 ABH is the same as for assault or battery. In this case, the defendant gave a lift in his car to a young woman. During the journey, he made unwanted sexual advances, touching the woman's clothes. Frightened that he was going to rape her, she jumped out of the moving car, injuring herself. It was held that the defendant had committed the *actus reus* of s.47 by touching her clothes — sufficient for battery — and this act had caused her to suffer actual bodily harm. The defendant argued that he lacked the *mens rea* of the offence, because he had neither intended to cause her actual bodily harm nor seen any risk of her suffering it as a result of his advances. This argument was rejected: the court held that the *mens rea* of battery was sufficient in itself, and there was no need for any extra *mens rea* regarding the actual bodily harm.

Malicious wounding or inflicting grievous bodily harm (s.20)

Section 20 created the offence of unlawfully and maliciously wounding or inflicting grievous bodily harm (GBH). The conduct element here is the same as for the more serious offence under s.18 (see below). A wound is defined as an injury that breaks both the outer and inner skin; a bruise or a burst blood vessel in the eye would not amount to a wound (see *C (a minor)* v *Eisenhower*, 1984). Grievous bodily harm is simply defined as 'really serious harm' (see *DPP* v *Smith*, 1961) or more simply as 'serious harm' (see *R* v *Saunders*, 1985). Typical GBH injuries which would require prompt hospital treatment include fractured arms or legs, any injury causing permanent disfigurement or disability or dislocated joints.

Biological GBH

This was established by the case of *R* v *Dica* (2004), which involved the conviction of a defendant for s.20 'biological' GBH after infecting two women with HIV. The Court of Appeal, having quashed his conviction and ordered a retrial, confirmed that injury by reckless infection *does* constitute a s.20 offence.

Mens rea *of s.20*

Section 20 requires either intention or recklessness to inflict some harm. This fault element was confirmed in the cases of *R* v *Mowatt* (1968) and *R* v *Grimshaw* (1984), which held that there is no need to prove recklessness as to wounding or grievous bodily harm, so long as the court is satisfied that the defendant was reckless as to *some physical harm* to some person, albeit of a minor character. As in all non-fatal offences where the *mens rea* includes recklessness, this is Cunningham or subjective recklessness — the prosecution must prove that the defendant did foresee that some physical harm might be caused.

Wounding or causing grievous bodily harm with intent (s.18)

This is a serious offence which carries a maximum sentence of life imprisonment. There are two forms of intent, the most common being 'intent to cause grievous bodily harm'. This requires proof that the defendant intended to cause a serious injury — **specific intent** (see *R* v *Nedrick*, 1986 and *R* v *Woollin*, 1998). This is either **direct intent**, where the defendant's aim or objective was to cause grievous bodily harm, or **oblique intent**, where the jury is satisfied that the defendant foresaw serious injury as virtually certain. In most cases of s.18 grievous bodily harm, the defendant will have used some form of weapon to inflict injuries on the victim, which makes it easier for the prosecution to prove the necessary intent. Where the prosecution fails to establish intention, the offence will be reduced to the lower s.20 offence, so long as recklessness as to causing some harm is proved.

Note that an alternative fault element is available for s.18, which relates to circumstances where a lawful arrest is being attempted and the intent is 'to prevent the lawful apprehension of any person'. The policy behind this element is that attacks on persons engaged in law enforcement are regarded as more serious. Under this, the defendant can be convicted if he or she pushes a police officer to prevent an arrest, and the officer falls and suffers a serious injury. There is no requirement that such serious results should have been foreseen or were even foreseeable. It is, however, a requirement in such cases that the prosecution proves that the defendant intended some harm, or was reckless as to whether harm was caused.

> **Examiner tip**
> Many students make the mistake of writing that the *mens rea* for s.20 is intention or recklessness as to causing serious harm/wounding, rather than 'some harm' which confuses this offence with s.18.

> **Examiner tip**
> There is no difference between the *actus reus* of s.20 and s.18. Some students make the mistake of writing that while the injuries are serious enough for s.20, they are not sufficiently serious for s.18.

Summary

Actus reus

The physical part of a crime — it must be voluntary (under the control of the defendant). It can also be an omission — a failure to act where the law imposes a duty — see relevant cases.

Causation:

- factual 'but for' rule, e.g. *R* v *White*
- legal rules — significant contribution/substantial and operating cause
- medical negligence cases, e.g. compare *R* v *Smith* and *R* v *Jordan*
- escape case, e.g. *R* v *Roberts*
- thin skull — take your victim as you find him, e.g. *R* v *Blaue*

Mens rea

The mental element of a crime.

- Intention:
  - direct intent — aim, purpose or objective, e.g. *R* v *Mohan*.
  - oblique intent — for specific intent offences only — for murder, defendant must recognise that death or serious injury is a virtually certain consequence of his voluntary act, e.g. *R* v *Nedrick*, *R* v *Woollin*, *R* v *Matthews and Alleyne*.
- Recklessness — subjective test. Defendant must have realised he was taking an unjustified risk, e.g. *R* v *Cunningham*.
- Coincidence of *actus reus* and *mens rea*: linked transaction or continuing act rule from *Thabo Meli* and *R* v *Le Brun*.

- Transferred malice: the intended victim and the actual victim are treated as if they were the same, e.g. *R* v *Latimer*.
- Strict liability offences:
  - No fault offences, mostly statutory with fines as penalties. Concern public safety — motoring, workplace safety etc. Cases include: *Callow* v *Tillstone*, *Harrow LBC* v *Shah*, *Alphacell* v *Woodward*.
  - Reasons for strict liability — easier to prove, save court time, provide better protection for public.

Non-fatal offences

These are summarised in Table 1 on p. 15. Typical injuries:

- **Battery:** no injury is required for this offence, but in practice, a very minor bruise, or slap, could be charged as battery.
- **Actual bodily harm (ABH):** bruising, a very minor fracture such as a broken finger.
- **Wounding:** under the Eisenhower definition, any cut which breaks both upper and lower layers of skin can be a wound. A very minor graze would more likely be ABH.
- **Grievous bodily harm (GBH):** fractured arms or legs, any injury causing permanent disfigurement or disability or dislocated joints. As a general rule, any injury which requires prompt hospital treatment.

Criminal courts

Classification of offences

There are three different classes of criminal offence:

- **Summary offences** — minor offences that can only be tried by magistrates (e.g. most road traffic offences, such as speeding).
- **Either-way offences** — offences which, as the name suggests, can be tried either by magistrates or in a Crown Court before a judge and jury (e.g. theft, burglary and s.47 ABH).
- **Indictable offences** — more serious offences that must be tried by a judge and jury in the Crown Court (e.g. murder, manslaughter, rape and causing GBH with intent).

Burden of proof and standard of proof

The most fundamental rule of English criminal law is that the defendant is presumed innocent until proven guilty. It is for the prosecution to prove this guilt, not for the defendant to prove his or her innocence. This principle was underlined in *Woolmington* v *DPP* (1935). Because of the serious consequences of a guilty verdict, including loss of freedom, the standard of proof is high — 'beyond reasonable doubt'. The judge will direct the jury to convict the defendant only if it is sure that he or she is guilty.

Magistrates' Courts

Magistrates' Courts hear applications for bail under the **Bail Act 1976**, which if granted means that the defendant is released from custody until the trial date. Under the Act, there is a presumption in favour of bail being granted because of the principle that the defendant is innocent until proven guilty. However, bail may be disallowed on the following grounds:

- the seriousness of the offence — bail is rarely granted in a murder case
- the possibility that the defendant may abscond (fail to turn up for trial)
- the fear that the defendant may interfere with witnesses
- the possibility that the defendant will reoffend

If bail is granted, it is usually unconditional. However, the court may impose conditions, such as the surrender of the defendant's passport, or a requirement that the defendant resides in a bail hostel until trial or reports to a police station at stated intervals.

Magistrates also hear applications for legal aid.

Crown Courts

The main jurisdiction of Crown Courts is to hear all indictable offences, such as murder, rape, robbery and the more serious either-way offences, where jurisdiction has been declined by magistrates or where the defendant has elected to be tried on indictment by a judge sitting with a jury. It also acts as an appeal court hearing cases from Magistrates' Courts.

Criminal court procedures

Magistrates' Court

- In a preliminary hearing, the court can hear applications for bail and legal aid.
- If the defendant is charged with an either-way offence, there will be a 'plea before venue' hearing.
- If the defendant opts for summary trial before magistrates, the court may decline jurisdiction and remit to the Crown Court. Otherwise, the court will set a trial date for when the case will be heard. If found guilty, the defendant will be sentenced, and there could be an appeal against sentence or conviction to the Crown Court.
- If the defendant is charged with an indictable offence, the case will automatically be remitted to the Crown Court under the **Crime and Disorder Act 1998**.

Examiner tip

In a general court procedure question, do not write too much on bail. Only mention Bail Act and the presumption in favour bail, and give one or two examples why bail may not be given.

Examiner tip

Read any 'procedural' question carefully — it will indicate with what type of offence the defendant has been charged. If it is a summary offence, *all* proceedings will take place before magistrates.

Crown Court

- There could be a pre-trial hearing before a circuit judge to determine whether there is a case to answer.
- If there is no such challenge by the defendant, or if the judge decides that there is sufficient evidence to justify a trial, the trial proceeds in the Crown Court before a judge and jury.
- If the defendant is convicted, the judge will sentence him or her — usually after a pre-sentence report has been obtained.

Court of Appeal (Criminal Division)

- The defendant can appeal against sentence or conviction with leave of the trial judge or a single Lord Justice of Appeal.
- Appeal against conviction can be made on the ground that the conviction is unsafe.
- Appeal against sentence can be made on the ground that the sentence was 'manifestly excessive'.
- The Court of Appeal may dismiss the appeal (uphold the conviction), quash the conviction, substitute a lower-level conviction (e.g. manslaughter instead of murder, or s.20 GBH rather than s.18 GBH) or order a retrial.

Supreme Court

- Final appeal against conviction only can be made to the Supreme Court only on the ground that the case raises a point of law 'of general public importance'.

Knowledge check 8

Under which Act must a defendant charged with an indictable offence be transferred to the Crown Court?

Sentencing

The current rules on sentencing are set out in the **Criminal Justice Act 2003**. Examiners will expect you to be aware of the changes made in this statute and to make appropriate reference to them. After a defendant has been convicted in a criminal case, the judge has to consider which aims of sentencing are appropriate to the case, the types of sentence available, any mitigating and aggravating factors, and the maximum sentence that may be imposed.

Aims of sentencing

Section 142 of the **Criminal Justice Act** defines the aims of sentencing as:

> ... the punishment of offenders; the reduction of crime (including its reduction by deterrence); the reform and rehabilitation of offenders; the protection of the public; and the making of reparation by offenders to persons affected by their offences.

Retribution

As an objective of sentencing, retribution simply means that a person who has broken the law shall be punished. However, it also includes the idea of 'just deserts' — that an individual offender should receive a punishment that reflects both the seriousness of the offence and his or her moral fault. Every type of sentence to some extent can be regarded as retributive.

Deterrence

Individual deterrence aims to prevent a particular offender from committing a further offence through fear of the punishment. General deterrence aims to deter other potential offenders. In sentencing one offender for a particular offence, it is hoped to deter other potential offenders from committing a like offence through fear of the punishment. Therefore, a general deterrent sentence will be an enhanced sentence. A policy of deterrence would promote unpleasant sentences and possibly longer sentences of imprisonment. It is clear from Home Office figures of **recidivism** (reoffending) that with 65% of those offenders who receive custodial sentences going on to reoffend within 2 years of release, this aspect of sentencing is currently unsuccessful. With low 'capture and conviction' rates at present, deterrence is highly unlikely to reduce either the amount of crime in general or the risk of an individual reoffending. In 2011 after the riots in London and other cities, heavy custodial sentences were imposed to act as a general deterrent.

Rehabilitation

The aim of rehabilitation is to reform the offender so that he or she will not reoffend. In practice, some sentencing options, such as community sentences, have a more obvious rehabilitative purpose than others (for example, custody or fines), in that they can be individualised to the circumstances of the particular offender. The goal is to improve an offender's character or behaviour in order to reintegrate him or her into society. Other rehabilitation sentencing options include educational and counselling services in prisons and the provision of specialist units to treat sexual and drug offenders.

Protection of the public

This aim requires that serious offenders — especially those who have committed violent crimes — should be imprisoned: custody is the only way in which the safety of the public can be guaranteed. The **Criminal Justice Act 1991** laid considerable emphasis on this aim for serious violent offenders, and this has been followed in the 2003 Act. Under s.227, extended sentences are possible, allowing the imposition of an extra period of custody where there is considered to be a significant risk of serious harm to the public. Up to 8 years could be added for a sexual offence, for example.

Reparation

Increasing attention is being given to the needs and views of victims, and there are already compensation orders that allow for offenders to be forced to make amends to the victim, usually through a financial payment. Clearly, this is only practicable where the offender has the necessary financial resources. Reparation could also be administered, if appropriate, through an imaginative community order providing for the offender to put right damage done — for instance by repairing something or painting over graffiti.

Types of sentence

Having considered which aim(s) would be most appropriate in a case, the judge must then consider the types of sentence that are open to him or her to impose.

Knowledge check 9

Why are community sentences more important in terms of offender rehabilitation?

Custodial sentences

This is the most serious form of sentence in English law — the deprivation of an individual's freedom by sending the offender to prison or to a young offenders' institution (depending on the age of the offender). Section 152 of the **Criminal Justice Act 2003** provides that, for custody to be imposed, the judge has to be satisfied that the offence is so serious that *only* custody can be justified.

Before the trial judge decides what length of sentence to impose in a particular case, he or she will seek guidance either from a Practice Statement from the Court of Appeal or from that court's consideration of a suitable tariff for such an offence. The **Sentencing Guidelines Council**, which was set up under the 2003 Act, can issue guidance on any aspect of sentencing, including tariffs, and courts are expected to take note of such guidance. The tariff will be the sentence appropriate for an 'average' example of the offence. All offences for which custody can be imposed have maximum sentences.

The judge usually has the discretion to decide on the length of a prison sentence, but there are also **mandatory sentences**, which are sentences that the judge must impose. Murder has an automatic life sentence, and under s.225 of the **Criminal Justice Act 2003**, an automatic life sentence is imposed if a person is convicted of a second serious violent or sexual offence.

A custodial sentence may be **suspended** — this means that the offender does not go to prison unless he or she reoffends during the period for which the sentence was suspended, which may not be longer than 2 years. Suspended sentences are now rare, and under s.118 of the 2003 Act they can only be imposed in exceptional circumstances.

Community sentences

Before the introduction of the **Criminal Justice Act 2003**, the courts could use individual community sentences, which they could combine with other sentences. The 2003 Act created one community order, under which any requirements can be incorporated that the court considers necessary. They can include all the previous community sentences and also some new requirements.

Each order should have appropriate requirements built in that reflect the seriousness of the offence. Examples are a curfew requirement, an exclusion requirement, a mental health treatment requirement and an alcohol treatment requirement or attendance on an anger-management course. There is also a supervision requirement, which puts the offender under the supervision of a probation officer for up to 3 years.

Fines

A fine is a sum of money ordered to be paid by the offender to the Crown. This is by far the most common form of punishment and is most often imposed for motoring offences and minor either-way offences.

Knowledge check 10

What elements may be included in a community sentence?

Discharges

Here the defendant is not sentenced as such, but if the discharge is conditional, he or she will be sentenced in respect of the original offence if he or she commits another offence within a specified period, which may not exceed 3 years. An absolute discharge would be appropriate in cases where the court feels that, although there is technically an offence, a prosecution should not have been brought, perhaps because the offence is too trivial or there are special circumstances affecting the offender.

Mitigating and aggravating factors

When passing sentence, the judge must consider both mitigating and aggravating factors.

Mitigating factors are pleaded on behalf of the defendant by counsel and could include:
- first conviction
- young offender
- guilty plea (usually results in a one-third reduction in sentence)
- offer to compensate the victim

Aggravating factors are issues that would normally result in a higher sentence being imposed. They include:
- vulnerable victim — either young or very old
- breach of trust
- offence committed while the defendant is on bail
- more than one defendant involved
- use of a weapon

The court may also want to refer to a **pre-sentence report** drawn up by the probation service, providing information on the defendant's background. This would be particularly relevant if the court was considering a custodial sentence or a community-based sentence. The court may ask for a medical or psychiatric report where this would be relevant.

Victim impact statements may be formally prepared and read to the court, and the court is obliged to have regard to these when considering sentence.

Maximum sentences

For the non-fatal offences that form the basis of questions in this unit, the maximum sentences are:
- assault or battery — 6 months
- s.47 ABH — 5 years
- s.20 GBH or wounding — 5 years
- s.18 GBH with intent — life imprisonment

Examiner tip

Read sentencing questions carefully to identify whether they are asking for aims, or types or factors of sentencing.

Summary

Criminal courts

Types of offence:
- summary — Magistrates' Courts only
- either-way — either Magistrates' Courts or Crown Court
- indictable — Crown Court only

Magistrates' Courts:
- preliminary hearing — bail and legal aid application
- plea before venue in either-way cases
- for indictable offences, transfer to Crown Court
- trial

Crown Court:
- pre-trial hearing
- trial by judge and jury

Court of Appeal: appeal by defendant against sentence or conviction

Supreme Court: appeal against conviction

Sentencing

Aims:
- retribution
- deterrence
- rehabilitation
- protection of society

Types:
- custodial
- community order
- financial — fines and compensation orders
- discharges — absolute and conditional

Factors:
- aggravating — make sentence more severe
- mitigating — make sentence more lenient

Introduction to tort

Liability in negligence

Negligence is by far the most important and most used tort in English law. A useful definition of tort is 'a wrong that entitles the injured party to claim compensation from the wrongdoer'. Another way of putting it is to say that someone is negligent if he or she acts carelessly towards another person, to whom there is a legal obligation to act carefully, and the carelessness causes the other person to suffer some kind of harm or loss.

Winfield writes that 'tortious liability arises from the breach of a duty primarily fixed by law', and it is here that we need to start our study of the tort of negligence. The word 'negligence' is defined by the *Shorter Oxford Dictionary* as 'want of attention to what ought to be done or looked after; lack of proper care in doing something'. In law, negligence is more tightly defined as 'breach of a duty of care that causes foreseeable loss or injury'. To understand its application and importance, it is necessary to study in turn each of the following three topics:
- duty of care
- breach of duty
- causation of foreseeable loss or injury

Duty of care

The tort of negligence owes its origins to the tale of a decomposing snail that was found in a ginger-beer bottle — *Donoghue* v *Stevenson* (1932). The claimant,

Mary Donoghue, went with a friend to a café, where her friend bought her a bottle of ginger beer. Donoghue opened it and poured some of the contents into a glass. When she finished this glass, she then poured the remainder of the bottle into the glass. At this point, the remains of a snail floated to the surface. This caused Donoghue to develop gastroenteritis and nervous shock, and she sought compensation from the ginger-beer manufacturer.

The case eventually reached the House of Lords, where Lord Atkin decided the case in her favour with his famous **neighbour principle**. In summary, this stated that 'you must take reasonable care to avoid acts or omissions which foreseeably could injure your neighbour', where neighbours are defined as 'persons who are so closely and directly affected by my act that I ought reasonably to have them in contemplation as being so affected when I am directing my mind to the acts or omissions'. In this case, the ginger-beer manufacturer should reasonably have had the claimant in mind when manufacturing and bottling the ginger beer.

This test clearly established that in order for a duty of care to be owed, there must be reasonable foresight of harm to persons who it is reasonable to foresee may be harmed by one's actions or omissions. Such 'duty' examples would obviously include cases involving doctor and patient, solicitor and client, car driver and other road users, employer and employee. However, the problem with this 'neighbour test' is that it has been used to create a duty of care in many less obvious situations, and the courts have therefore had to develop further guidelines to impose some limits on the scope of this principle. The modern approach comes from the case of *Caparo Industries plc* v *Dickman* (1990), which laid down what is called the **incremental approach**. This asks three questions:

- Was the damage or loss foreseeable?
- Is there sufficient proximity (a sufficiently close relationship) between the wrongdoer and the victim?
- Is it just, fair and reasonable to impose a duty of care?

If the answer to all these questions is 'yes', a duty of care is established. However, the claimant also needs to determine that the defendant breached that duty of care, that his or her loss or injury was caused by the breach of duty, and that such a loss was reasonably foreseeable (not too remote).

Foreseeability

The issue of foreseeability simply means that a reasonable person would have foreseen some damage or harm to the claimant at the time of the alleged negligence. A doctor's failure to diagnose a common medical problem will foreseeably lead to complications; a car driver's mistake will foreseeably cause a road accident; a mining company that does not observe safety laws will foreseeably have employees injured in accidents, and so on.

The case of *Langley* v *Dray* (1998) provides a clear illustration of this rule. The claimant was a police officer who was injured in a crash while pursuing a defendant driving a stolen car. The Court of Appeal ruled that the defendant knew he was being pursued by the claimant. It followed that in increasing his speed and exposing himself to a higher risk, he ought to have foreseen that the claimant would increase his speed

> **Examiner tip**
> Although an 'explanation' question on duty of care can be answered effectively by explaining the *Caparo* incremental approach, some reference to the 'neighbour principle' is always creditworthy.

Examiner tip

In explaining the meaning of duty of care, state it is an objective test, and that it only requires there to be reasonable foreseeability of *some* harm or property damage occurring if the defendant does not take reasonable care. The precise form of injury or damage need not be foreseeable.

accordingly and expose himself to the same risk. Another helpful case is *Kent* v *Griffiths* (2000) in which a doctor called for an ambulance to take a patient suffering from a severe asthma attack to hospital immediately. The ambulance failed to arrive within a reasonable time and there was no good reason for the delay. The patient suffered a heart attack which would not have occurred if the ambulance had arrived in time. It was held that it was reasonably foreseeable that the claimant would suffer some harm from this delay.

Proximity

Proximity means closeness in terms of time, space or relationship, and in many cases the issues of proximity and that of foreseeability will be similar. For instance, in a road traffic accident, the fact that the injured party could foreseeably be harmed will itself be proof of proximity. However, the case of *Bourhill* v *Young* (1943) is interesting in this context. The pregnant claimant was descending from a tram when she heard a motor accident. She did not actually witness it but later saw blood on the road and suffered nervous shock and a miscarriage. Although it was reasonably foreseeable that some people would suffer harm as a result of the defendant's negligent driving, injury to the specific claimant was not foreseeable as she was not in the immediate vicinity of the accident, only hearing but not seeing it. Her action therefore failed.

Knowledge check 11

Why was Mrs Bourhill unsuccessful in her claim for negligence?

The case of *McLoughlin* v *O'Brian* (1983) usefully illustrates the issue of relationship within proximity. In this case, the claimant arrived at the hospital where the victims were being treated so she was not proximate in terms of the accident itself, but because of her close relationship to the victims — wife and mother — she succeeded in her claim.

The 'just, fair and reasonable' test

This test is usually referred to as the **'policy test'**, under which judges are able to limit the extent of this tort. The principal reason for this judicial discretion is the argument that the floodgates would be opened if claims of liability were determined simply by reference to foreseeability. American judge Cardozo CJ referred to this danger when he warned of 'liability in an indeterminate amount for an indeterminate time to an indeterminate class'.

A good case to illustrate the use by courts of this discretion is *Mulcahy* v *Ministry of Defence* (1996). The defendant was a soldier who had served in the Gulf War, where he had suffered damage to his hearing when a fellow soldier fired a howitzer shell. The Court of Appeal held that, although both factors of foreseeabilty and proximity were present, the facts of the case required them to consider this as a policy issue — effectively to ask whether it was just, fair and reasonable to impose a duty of care on the Ministry of Defence in battlefield situations. Unsurprisingly, it was decided that no such duty of care could be imposed. Another good case example is *Hill* v *Chief Constable of West Yorkshire*. Here, the claimant was the mother of the last murder victim of the Yorkshire Ripper and she sued the police for their earlier failure to charge Peter Sutcliffe. The House of Lords held that there were sound policy reasons to deny liability in this case as it could lead the police to carry out their work with the aim of preventing liability which would adversely affect their performance.

The application of this test can also be seen in the following types of case:

- nervous shock — *Alcock* v *Chief Constable of South Yorkshire* (1992)
- pure economic loss — *Hedley Byrne* v *Heller* (1963)
- public organisations exercising a statutory duty — *X* v *Bedfordshire County Council* (1995)

Breach of duty

Once the claimant has shown that the defendant owed him or her a duty of care, it is necessary to prove that the defendant breached this duty. In other words, it must be proved that the defendant acted carelessly. For example, in *Donoghue* v *Stevenson*, the defendant allowed the snail to get into the ginger-beer bottle.

The key question that the court asks in order to determine whether this duty has been breached is: 'Did the defendant behave as the reasonable person would have in these circumstances?' This test was described well by Alderson LJ in *Blyth* v *Birmingham Waterworks Co.* (1856): 'Negligence [meaning 'breach of duty'] is the omission to do something which a reasonable man...would do, or doing something which a prudent and reasonable man would not do.'

The standard is therefore objective — any personal difficulties or disabilities that might be encountered by the specific defendant cannot be taken into account. This is made clear in the case of *Nettleship* v *Weston* (1971). The claimant gave the defendant driving lessons. On the third lesson, the car struck a lamp post and the claimant was injured. It was decided that the defendant, although a learner driver, would be judged by the standard of the average competent driver: 'The learner driver may be doing his best, but his incompetent best is not good enough. He must drive in as good a manner as a driver of skill, experience and care.'

Professional persons

Where a particular defendant has a professional skill and the case involves the exercise of that skill, the court will expect the defendant to show that he or she has the degree of competence usually to be expected of an ordinary skilled member of that profession. This means that a general practitioner is only expected to exercise the normal level of skill of a GP, not that of a senior consultant heart surgeon. The leading cases here are both medical — *Bolam* v *Friern Hospital Management Committee* (1957) and *Bolitho* v *City and Hackney Health Authority Committee* (1998).

In *Bolam*, it was held that 'a doctor is not guilty of negligence if he has acted in accordance with a practice accepted as proper by a responsible body of medical opinion skilled in that particular art'.

Children

The conduct of a child defendant is compared to the standard of conduct to be expected of a reasonable child of the same age as the defendant. In *Mullins* v *Richards* (1998) two 15-year-old schoolgirls were playing with plastic rulers and when one broke, a piece of plastic blinded one girl. As it was held that a reasonable 15-year-old girl would not have foreseen this risk of harm, there was no liability.

Knowledge check 12

Explain the meaning of the 'floodgates argument'.

Examiner tip

This test tends to be more poorly explained than the other two, so it is important to explain a relevant case such as *Mulcahy* effectively.

Knowledge check 13

Why was the defendant in *Nettleship* v *Weston* held liable, even though she was only a learner driver?

Examiner tip

In any problem-solving question dealing with the issue of breach of duty, the central question is whether or not the defendant acted as 'the reasonable person' would have acted in the same circumstances.

Tests to determine breach of duty

To assist the court in deciding whether the defendant has breached his or her duty of care, certain straightforward tests have been established. Each test is clearly illustrated by a case; you therefore need to be familiar both with these rules and with the accompanying cases.

Degree of probability that harm will be done

Care must be taken in respect of a risk, where it is reasonably foreseeable that harm or injury may occur. Nearly all human actions or omissions involve the possibility of harm, but not every risky act will be regarded as negligent.

In *Bolton* v *Stone* (1951), a batsman hit a ball that struck and injured the claimant, who was standing on the road outside the cricket ground. Evidence showed that a ball had only been hit out of the ground on six occasions in the previous 30 years, and on no previous occasion had anyone been injured. The defendant owner of the ground was found not to have been negligent, as a reasonable person would have been justified in disregarding the risk.

Compare this case with *Haley* v *London Electricity Board* (1964). Here, the defendants left a hammer on the pavement to warn people of excavations. The claimant, who was blind, tripped over it and was injured. It was held that although the warning was sufficient for sighted people, it was not adequate for a blind person. The number of blind people was sufficiently large to make them a group that the defendants ought reasonably to have had in contemplation.

Magnitude of likely harm

The court considers not only the risk of any harm but also how serious that harm could potentially be.

In *Paris* v *Stepney Borough Council* (1951), the claimant, who was blind in one eye, was employed as a mechanic in the defendants' garage, where his job included welding. It was not normal to supply goggles, and when a piece of metal flew into the claimant's good eye, he became completely blind. The defendants were held to be liable, although they would not have been liable to a person with normal sight. The greater risk to the claimant meant that greater precautions than normal should have been taken.

Cost and practicality of preventing the risk

Once the court has identified a risk as reasonably foreseeable, the next issue is whether the defendant should have taken precautions against that risk. If the cost of taking precautions to eliminate the risk is completely disproportionate to the extent of the risk itself, the defendant will not be held liable.

In *Latimer* v *AEC Ltd* (1953), a factory was flooded, and the owner used sawdust to reduce the effects of the flooding. However, some areas of the factory floor remained slippery and, as a result, an employee was injured when he fell. The owner was held not to have breached his duty of care, because the only way to have avoided

Knowledge check 14

Why was the defendant in *Bolton* v *Stone* not held to be liable?

that risk was to have closed the factory completely. In the circumstances, this was out of proportion to the level of risk involved. (Note that *Bolton* v *Stone*, above, also illustrates this test effectively).

Potential benefits of the risk

In some cases, the court has to weigh up whether there are risks that have potential benefits for society. In *Daborn* v *Bath Tramways Motor Co. Ltd* (1946), it was held that: 'If all trains were restricted to a speed of 5 m.p.h., there would be fewer rail accidents, but our national life would be intolerably slowed down. The purpose to be served, if sufficiently important, justifies the assumption of abnormal risk.'

In *Watt* v *Hertfordshire County Council* (1954), the claimant fireman was injured by a heavy jack that had been loaded quickly (but not secured) into the fire engine, in order to respond to an emergency call involving a road accident victim. It was held that in these circumstances, the risk involved was not so great as to prohibit an attempt to save life.

Res ipsa loquitur

This means literally 'the thing speaks for itself' and refers to situations where the judge is entitled to infer that the defendant's negligence caused the event, in the absence of any explanation from the defendant. In *Scott* v *London and St Katherine Docks Co.* (1865), the claimant, a customs officer, was injured by some bags of sugar falling on him while standing near the door of the defendant's warehouse. At the first trial, the judge directed the jury to find for the defendant on the grounds that there was no evidence of negligence put forward by the claimant. However, a retrial was ordered, in which the doctrine of *res ipsa loquitur* was first made:

> There must be reasonable evidence of negligence. But where the thing is shown to be under the management of the defendant or his servants, and the accident is such as in the ordinary course of things does not happen if those who have the management use proper care, it affords reasonable evidence, in the absence of explanation by the defendant, that the accident arose from want of care.

There are three separate requirements that must be satisfied for *res ipsa loquitur* to be accepted:

(1) The doctrine is dependent on the absence of explanation. This means that if the court finds from the evidence how and why the occurrence took place, the rule will not apply (*Barkway* v *South Wales Transport Co. Ltd,* 1950).

(2) The harm must be of such a kind that it does not ordinarily happen if proper care is taken. The courts have applied this doctrine to things falling from buildings and to accidents resulting from defective machines, apparatus or vehicles (*Scott* v *London and St Katherine Docks Co.*, 1865).

(3) What caused the accident must be within the exclusive control of the defendant. If the defendant is not in control, the doctrine does not apply. In *Gee* v *Metropolitan Railway Co.* (1873), a few minutes after a local train had started its journey, the claimant leaned against the carriage door, which flew open. This was held to be evidence of negligence, whereas in *Easson* v *LNER Co.* (1944), the claimant's

Knowledge check 15

What are the three requirements which must be satisfied for the *res ipsa* rule to come into effect?

action failed because it was held that 'it is impossible to say that the doors of an express train travelling from Edinburgh to London are continuously under the control of the railway company'.

Damage or causation of foreseeable loss or injury

The claimant must be able to prove both that his or her damage or injury was caused by the defendant's breach of duty and that the damage or injury was not remote, i.e. it was reasonably foreseeable.

'But for' test

The first question that needs to be asked is: 'But for the defendant's breach of duty, would the damage or injury have occurred?' The leading case is *Barnett* v *Chelsea and Kensington Hospital Management Committee* (1968). The claimant's husband attended the defendants' hospital, complaining of severe stomach pain and vomiting. The doctor in the Accident and Emergency department refused to examine him and he was sent home. Five hours later he died from arsenic poisoning. The defendants clearly owed the man a duty of care and were in breach by failing to examine him. However, they were held not liable because the facts established that, even if he had been examined, he would have died before diagnosis and treatment could have been carried out. As the man would have died regardless of the breach, the hospital's breach of duty was not the cause of his death.

Remoteness of damage

Damages might not be awarded, even where the claimant has established that the defendant's breach of duty (negligence) factually caused the damage or injury. It must be established that the damage was not too remote. The present rule of law on remoteness of damage was laid down in the Privy Council case of *Overseas Tankship (UK) Ltd* v *Morts Dock and Engineering Co.* (1961). This is better known as *The Wagon Mound No. 1* case, after the name of the ship concerned. This case effectively overruled the case of *Re Polemis* (1921), where it had been held that the defendant was liable for all direct consequences of the breach — this test was held to be too wide. Instead, the *Wagon Mound* case established a test of reasonable foreseeability.

The defendant negligently discharged fuel oil into Sydney harbour, and the oil spread to the claimant's wharf, where welding operations were taking place. The facts are clear — because of the negligence of employees, bunker oil leaked from the Wagon Mound and spread as a slick across Sydney harbour. This slick spread to a wharf owned by the claimants where it caused some damage to a slipway but a few days later, the oil was ignited by sparks from a welder who was working on a ship repair and more substantial damage was caused to the slipway. On appeal to the Judicial Committee of the Privy Council, it was decided that no damages were recoverable for the fire damage caused to the wharf on the ground that this damage was too remote a consequence of the original breach — it was held that the type of damage or harm had to be reasonably foreseeable at the time of the breach.

The decision in this case was affirmed in the case of *Doughty* v *Turner Manufacturing Co. Ltd* (1964), which held that the defendant was not liable for the burns suffered by the claimant when an asbestos cover was accidentally dropped into some molten liquid. The resulting eruption of the liquid was too remote.

In addition to these, there are other rules that need to be learned. The first is that, if the kind of damage suffered is reasonably foreseeable, it does not matter that the damage actually occurred in an unforeseeable way. This principle is clearly illustrated by the case of *Hughes* v *Lord Advocate* (1963), where the defendants had erected a tent over a manhole and surrounded the tent with paraffin lamps. The 10-year-old claimant dropped one of these lamps down the hole. Owing to an unusual combination of circumstances, there was an explosion and the claimant was badly burned. Despite the defendants' argument that the explosion of the lamp was too remote, the House of Lords held they were liable. The question was asked: 'What kind of injury was foreseeable as a result of the breach of duty (leaving the hole unguarded)?' The answer was 'burns'. 'What kind of injury had occurred?' Again the answer was 'burns'. The damage was therefore not too remote.

Another case that can be used to illustrate this rule is *Jolley* v *Sutton London Borough Council* (2000). The claimant was a 14-year-old boy who had been seriously injured when he had tried to repair an old boat that he had found abandoned in a council park. While it was on a jack, the boat had fallen on him. The defendants admitted that the boat should have been removed from the park but denied liability for the accident, claiming that boys playing on the boat was foreseeable but the attempt to repair it was not. The Court of Appeal agreed with that argument, but the House of Lords reversed the decision — it was foreseeable that children would in some way 'get involved' with the boat. It was not necessary for the defendants to foresee the boy's attempt to repair it, using a jack to lift it.

The second rule that also needs to be learned is the 'thin skull' rule, which states, as noted on p. 10, that when the possibility of damage is foreseeable, defendants must take their victims as they find them as regards physical characteristics. This means that the defendant will be liable when the injuries to the claimant are more serious than might have been anticipated because of factors peculiar to the victim.

The leading case that shows how this rule works in practice is *Smith* v *Leech Brain and Co. Ltd* (1961). The claimant's husband was employed by the defendants. His work required him to lower articles into a tank containing molten metal. An accident occurred and Mr Smith was struck on the lip by a piece of molten metal. He later died of cancer, which was triggered by the burn. Lord Parker CJ held:

> The test is not whether these defendants could reasonably have foreseen that a burn would cause cancer and that Mr Smith would die. The question is whether these defendants could reasonably foresee the type of injury which he suffered, namely the burn. What, in the particular case, is the amount of damage which he suffers as a result of that burn, depends on the characteristics and constitution of the victim.

Knowledge check 16

Why, despite the fact that an explosion was held to be unforeseeable, was the defendant held liable for damages in *Hughes* v *Lord Advocate*?

Examiner tip

When explaining remoteness of damages, include the tests from *Hughes* v *Lord-Advocate* and *Smith* v *Leech Brain* to ensure a 'sound response'.

Summary

Duty of care

- Neighbour principle: *Donoghue* v *Stevenson* — 'take reasonable care to avoid acts or omissions which you can reasonably foresee would be likely to injure your neighbour'.
- *Caparo* v *Dickman*: incremental approach.
- Foreseeability: objective test — a reasonable person would have foreseen some damage or harm to the claimant when the negligence occurred, e.g. *Langley* v *Dray*, *Kent* v *Griffiths*.
- Proximity: closeness in terms of time, space or relationship, e.g. *Bourhill* v *Young*, *McLoughlin* v *O'Brian*.
- Just, fair and reasonable: policy test — to prevent 'floodgates' opening, e.g. *Mulcahy* v *MoD*, *Hill* v *Chief Constable of West Yorkshire*.

Breach of duty

- Reasonable man test: did the defendant behave as the reasonable man would have in the same circumstances? Objective test, so no account taken of personal circumstances except age, e.g. *Nettleship* v *Weston*, *Blyth* v *Birmingham Waterworks Co.*, *Mullins* v *Richards*.
- Professional persons: defendant expected to show the same degree of competence usually to be expected of an ordinary skilled member of that profession, e.g. *Bolam* v *Friern Barnet Hospital Management Committee*, *Bolitho* v *City and Hackney Health Authority*.
- Risk factors:
  - probability of harm, e.g. *Bolton* v *Stone*
  - magnitude of possible harm, e.g. *Paris* v *Stepney Borough Council*

- cost and practicality of taking precautions, e.g. *Latimer* v *AEC Ltd*
  - potential benefits of taking risk, e.g. *Watt* v *Hertfordshire County Council*
- *Res ipsa loquitur*: 'the thing speaks for itself', e.g. *Scott* v *London and St Katherine Docks Co.*:
  - The doctrine is dependent on the absence of explanation.
  - The harm must be of such a kind that it does not ordinarily happen if proper care is taken.
  - What caused the accident must be within the exclusive control of the defendant. If the defendant is not in control, the doctrine does not apply.

Damage or causation of foreseeable loss or injury

- Factual 'but for' test, e.g. *Barnett* v *Chelsea and Kensington HMC*.
- Remoteness of damage: defendant not liable if damage too remote. The test is: was the kind of damage or harm suffered by the claimant reasonably foreseeable at the time of the breach? E.g. *Wagon Mound No.1*, *Doughty* v *Turner Manufacturing Co. Ltd*.
- Type of damage: if the kind of damage suffered is reasonably foreseeable, it does not matter that the damage actually occurred in an unforeseeable way, e.g. *Hughes* v *Lord Advocate*.
- Thin skull test: the defendant will be liable when the injuries to the claimant are more serious than might have been anticipated because of factors peculiar to the victim, e.g. *Smith* v *Leech Brain and Co. Ltd*.

Damages

The purpose of damages is to put the claimant in the position in which he or she was before the tortious act, as far as can be achieved by money. To calculate the award, damages are divided into two kinds — **special damages** and **general damages**.

Special damages

These comprise quantifiable financial losses up to the date of trial and are assessed separately from other awards because the exact amount to be claimed is known at the time of the trial. The major types of damages are as follows:

- **Loss of earnings.** This is calculated from the date of the tort to the trial.
- **Medical expenses.** These cover any services, treatment or medical appliances, or the unpaid services of relatives or friends. Only such expenses as are considered reasonable by the court are recoverable. In *Cunningham* v *Harrison* (1973), the claimant said that he needed a housekeeper and two nurses to live in his home and look after him. The court refused to allow this claim as it was considered unreasonably large. However, in *Donnelly* v *Joyce* (1972) the claimant was successful in claiming the financial loss that his mother had suffered as a result of having to care for him.
- **Expenses to cover special facilities.** These can cover the cost of special living accommodation. The measure of damages here is the sum spent to obtain the special facility and its running costs. In *Povey* v *Rydal School* (1970), the claimant received an award to cover the cost of a special hydraulic lift to take a wheelchair in and out of a car. A large amount of money can be spent to adapt a house for people with particular disabilities.

Knowledge check 17

What is meant by special damages?

General damages

This term covers all losses that are not capable of exact quantification, and they are further divided into **pecuniary** and **non-pecuniary** damages.

Pecuniary damages

The major type of pecuniary damages is future loss of earnings. The courts calculate this amount using the **multiplicand** (a sum to represent the claimant's annual net lost earnings) and the **multiplier** (a notional figure that represents a number of years for which the claimant was likely to have worked). These are multiplied together in order to calculate the future losses. The multiplier is arbitrary — it can never be precise and is calculated by looking at previous cases. Even in the case of a young wage earner, the maximum multiplier used is 18, because it is intended to take into account the possibility that the claimant may lose his or her job or retire early.

The expectation is that the claimant will invest any money received as a lump sum and use the income, and possibly some of the capital, to cover living expenses during the years when he or she would have been earning, so that by the time of retirement the whole of the sum awarded will be exhausted.

As victims of accidents often receive financial support from several sources in addition to tort damages (e.g. social security benefits, sick pay and private insurance), amounts are deducted from the damages award to account for these.

However, the claimant is entitled to an award to cover the cost of future care, such as nursing requirements and physiotherapy.

Non-pecuniary damages

The main types of non-pecuniary damages are as follows:
- **Pain and suffering.** Compensation for pain and suffering is subjective, as they are impossible to measure in terms of money. However, an award will be made to cover nervous shock and physical pain and suffering. It is important to achieve consistency between the awards made to different claimants who suffer

similar injuries. The Judicial Studies Board sets tariffs to govern the fixing of the appropriate figure. However, each tariff provides for a range of possible awards, and a claimant who can show that the injury has had a particular impact upon his or her life may be able to recover at the high end of the range.

- **Loss of amenity.** The claimant is entitled to claim damages if his or her injury has led to the inability to carry out everyday activities and to enjoy life. This includes, for example, inability to run or walk, play sport or play a musical instrument, and impairment of the senses. Such awards are assessed objectively and are thus independent of the victim's knowledge of his or her fate. In *West* v *Shephard* (1964), the claimant was 41 when she suffered a severe head injury. Although she could not speak, there was evidence from her eye movements that she understood her predicament, and so she received a high award for loss of amenity.
- **Damages for the injury itself.** Injuries are itemised, and specified sums are awarded for these on the basis of precedents.

Knowledge check 18

What are the three types of non-pecuniary damages?

Provisional damages

The general rule is that only one award of damages can be made. If damage turns out to be more serious than was anticipated at the time of the award, no further action is available to the claimant, and this can cause obvious hardship in personal injury cases. Under s.32a of the **Supreme Court Act 1981**, the court has power to make a provisional award that allows the claimant to return to court should further anticipated serious deterioration occur. This power is not commonly used.

Structured settlements

These are the result not of legislation but of practical moves by lawyers and insurers to circumvent the usual lump-sum payments and increase the benefit to the claimant. The claimant receives, instead of one lump sum, an initial payment which covers losses to that date and then regular payments as a pension which will last for the rest of the claimant's life. Such a settlement has to be agreed by the parties — it cannot be imposed by the judge.

Examiner tip

Ensure that you understand the difference between special and general damages. Confusing these will result in marks being lost.

Mitigation of loss

The claimant is required to take reasonable steps to mitigate (reduce) his or her loss. The defendant will not be liable to compensate the claimant for any losses that could have been prevented by taking such steps.

Summary

- Purpose of damages: to compensate the claimant.
- Special damages: quantifiable losses to time of trial — include medical costs and loss of earnings.
- General damages:
  - Pecuniary: loss of future earnings — multiplicand figure to represent average future annual earning times multiplier. Future medical costs.
  - Non-pecuniary: pain and suffering, the injury itself, loss of amenity (enjoyment of life).
- Structured settlement: one lump sum plus future regular payments — must be agreed by both parties.

Civil courts

This section is relevant to both Tort and Contract. In both sections you will have to answer a question covering things like the procedure likely to be followed before trial, the court and track the case would probably be assigned to and the possibility of using ADR as an alternative to court proceedings.

Burden of proof and standard of proof

In almost all civil cases, the burden of proof rests on the claimant to prove his or her case against the defendant. The standard of proof is 'on the balance of probabilities' — a much lower standard than that in criminal cases, where the prosecution has to prove its case beyond reasonable doubt.

County Courts

There are more than 300 County Courts in England and Wales, which handle the majority of civil cases. They have a wide jurisdiction covering tort, contract cases, land law disputes, undefended divorce actions and other family law cases, such as adoption. The maximum financial limit for claims in the County Court is £50,000.

Cases may only be heard in the County Court within whose local jurisdiction the defendant lives or, if the defendant is a company, the registered office of the company is based.

Cases are directed to one of three separate 'tracks' under the Civil Procedure Rules (CPR):
- small claims track — claims for up to £5,000 (£1,000 for personal injury)
- fast track — claims worth between £5,000 and £25,000
- multi-track — all cases worth more than £25,000. Generally, claims for more than £50,000 are allocated to the High Court

High Court

Complex civil cases involving claims for large amounts of money are usually directed to the High Court.

The High Court is based in London but can also sit in major cities. It is organised into three divisions:
- The **Queen's Bench Division** is the largest and busiest division, and hears most contract and tort cases.
- The **Chancery Division** hears cases involving tax disputes and company law.
- The **Family Division** hears defended divorce actions and other matrimonial cases. It is also concerned with the welfare of children under the **Children Act 1989**; judges may have to decide cases involving adoption, guardianship and the custody of and access to children.

> **Knowledge check 19**
> Which court would hear the following and which track would be used in each case:
> (a) a claim for personal injury damages of £16,000?
> (b) a claim for property damages of £65,000?

Opportunity for alternative dispute resolution

Under the Civil Procedure Rules, the courts now have a clear duty 'actively to manage cases justly'. This includes encouraging the parties to use an alternative dispute resolution (ADR) procedure if the court considers that appropriate. If one of the parties unreasonably refuses to consider this option, the court has the power to disallow legal costs in the subsequent court case. This was the result in *Dunnett* v *Railtrack* (2002).

- The court does not have the power to order reluctant litigants to mediate, and to do so would be a breach of Article 6 rights — the right to a fair trial before an independent tribunal.
- The court's role is limited to encouraging the parties to enter ADR.
- Where a party reasonably believes that its case is 'watertight', it may be justified in refusing mediation.
- All those involved in litigation should routinely consider with their clients whether their disputes are suitable for ADR.
- While most cases are suitable for ADR, there should not be a presumption in favour of it.

Procedure to trial

The claimant must first send details of his or her claim to the defendant. If the defendant rejects the claim or fails to reply to it, the claimant then makes a formal claim in the County Court using a Form N1. This form contains particulars of the claim, together with details of the claimant and defendant, and the amount of money claimed.

If no defence to the claim is lodged by the defendant, default judgement will be made in favour of the claimant. If a defence is lodged, the case will be directed by the court to the appropriate 'track', depending on the value of the claim. If it is allocated to the small claims track, the procedure will be a less formal hearing before a district judge who, in effect, acts as an arbitrator. If allocated to the fast track, there will be a preliminary hearing to lay down a timetable for procedural matters such as discovery of documents by both sides, and a trial date will be set within 30 weeks. The trial will be heard by a circuit judge or Recorder. Multi-track cases will be allocated to the County Court or High Court, depending on the claim value or level of legal complexity of the case. Again, there will be a case-management hearing where the judge will impose a timetable for procedural issues to be determined.

Appeals procedure

It is always open to the unsuccessful party in a civil case to try to appeal the decision of the trial judge to a higher court, but leave to appeal must be obtained. In most appeal cases, the grounds for appeal relate to legal issues rather than arguments about the facts of the case. If the appellant is successful in his or her appeal, the decision of the trial judge may be overturned or damages may be reduced. The routes for appeal are:

- from small claims cases to a single circuit judge in the County Court
- from fast-track cases in the County Court to a single High Court judge

Knowledge check 20

How are multi-track cases allocated to either County Courts or the High Court?

- from multi-track cases in the County Court to the Court of Appeal (Civil Division), presided over by two Lord Justices of Appeal
- from the High Court to the Court of Appeal (Civil Division), presided over by three Lord Justices of Appeal
- from the Court of Appeal to the Supreme Court, provided leave to appeal has been granted, either by the Court of Appeal itself or after application to the Supreme Court; such leave will only be given if the case raises issues of 'general public importance'

Summary

- Small claims track: claims for up to £5,000 (£1,000 for personal injury) — County Court Small Claims arbitration.
- Fast track: claims worth between £5,000 and £25,000 — County Court.
- Multi-track: all cases worth more than £25,000. Generally, claims for more than £50,000 are allocated to the High Court.
- Parties may be encouraged to use ADR to resolve disputes. If a dispute is unresolved by negotiation, a formal claim is made by completing Form NI.

- Appeals may be made as follows:
  - from small claims cases to a single circuit judge in the County Court
  - from fast-track cases in the County Court to a single High Court judge
  - from multi-track cases in the County Court to the Court of Appeal (Civil Division)
  - from the High Court to the Court of Appeal (Civil Division)
  - from the Court of Appeal to the Supreme Court

Introduction to contract

A contract can be defined as a legally binding agreement. In other words, it is an agreement that is recognised as having legal consequences.

Formation of contract

In order to be valid, a contract must meet certain conditions, and these have to be present when it is formed. There can be several parties to a contract, and contracts can be made by individuals, groups or organisations. Most contracts involve one party making an offer and another party indicating acceptance either verbally or in writing. These are known as **bilateral contracts** because for the contract to be valid, both parties must promise something. There are also **unilateral contracts**, where one party makes an offer but acceptance is through the performance of an act rather than through a formal indication of acceptance.

A valid contract requires one party to make an **offer** and another party to accept that offer. This then becomes an **agreement**.

Offer

An offer has been defined as an expression of willingness to contract on certain terms, made with the intention that it will become binding on acceptance.

An offer can be specific — made to one person or a group of people — in which case it can only be accepted by that person or group. However, an offer can also be general and not limited in whom it is directed at. An offer of a reward is a good example. This could be accepted by anyone who meets the conditions. An offer may have time limits attached, in which case it can only be accepted during that time period. Offers without time limits are open for a 'reasonable time'.

The following are offers:

- **Reward posters/advertisements**. In some circumstances, reward posters and advertisements can constitute offers. Offers must be firm, capable of being accepted and clear in requiring certain conditions to be fulfilled. This was established in *Carlill* v *Carbolic Smoke Ball Co.* (1893). The Carbolic Smoke Ball Company issued a newspaper advertisement in which it said it would pay £100 to any person who contracted influenza after using one of its smoke balls in a specified manner for a specified period. It also stated that it had deposited £1,000 with a named bank, to show its sincerity in the matter. Mrs Carlill was the customer who held the company to its word. Believing the accuracy of the advertisement, she purchased one of the balls and used it as directed — but contracted influenza nevertheless. She claimed for her £100 and then sued when the company refused to pay her. The Court of Appeal found in favour of Mrs Carlill. This is an unusual case, but it does show that an advert can amount to an offer if the wording makes it clear that it is intended to be an offer.
- **Promotional campaigns.** A supermarket might encourage customers to buy one product and get another product free, or it might offer two items for the price of one. As with reward posters, all that is required is that certain conditions are fulfilled.

Further rules about offers

Offers are also subject to the following rules:

- **The offer must be certain.** This means that its terms must be clear and definite, without any ambiguity. For example, in *Guthing* v *Lynn* (1831), a promise to pay an extra £5 'if the horse is lucky' was considered too vague to constitute an offer.
- **The offer may be made by any method.** There is no requirement that an offer is in a particular form. It can be made in writing, verbally or by conduct (e.g. by picking up an item and taking it to the cash desk).
- **The offer can be made to anyone.** It can be made to an individual, a group, a company or an organisation, and even, as in *Carlill* v *Carbolic Smoke Ball Co.*, to the whole world. Lord Justice Lindley commented in *Carlill*: 'The offer is to anybody who performs the conditions named in the advertisement. Anybody who does perform the conditions accepts the offer.'
- **The offer must be communicated.** A person cannot accept what he or she does not know about. In practice, this is not likely to happen very often, but one example might be an offer of a reward for the return of a missing dog. If someone finds the dog and returns it, but that person did not know about the reward, then technically he or she is not entitled to the reward because the offer was never received and therefore cannot be accepted.
- **The offer must still be in existence when it is accepted.** If a time limit is attached the offer will cease to exist on expiry of the time limit. An offer may also have been terminated.

AQA AS Law

Termination of offers

An offer can be brought to an end at any point before acceptance and in a number of ways:

- **Acceptance/refusal.**
- **Counter-offer.** In *Hyde* v *Wrench* (1840), Wrench offered to sell his farm to Hyde for £1,000. Hyde offered to pay £950, which Wrench rejected. When Hyde then tried to accept the original offer, it was held that his counter-offer of £950 had ended that offer. This case confirms that all the terms of an offer must be accepted, and an attempt to change any of them becomes a counter-offer.
- **Revocation.** Revocation (withdrawal of the offer) must be communicated, though this could be by a third party, as in *Dickinson* v *Dodds* (1876). The revocation must be received before the acceptance is made. In *Byrne* v *Van Tienhoven* (1880), Van Tienhoven wrote to Byrne on 1 October, making an offer, but changed his mind and wrote again to Byrne on 8 October, withdrawing his offer. However, Byrne accepted the offer in a telegram on 11 October, before he received the revocation letter, and therefore the acceptance was valid.
- **Lapse of time.** Where no time limit is specified, the offer will remain open for a reasonable time. What is a reasonable time will depend on the circumstances. For example, an offer to sell perishable goods may lapse in a few days, while an offer to sell land would last considerably longer. In *Ramsgate Victoria Hotel* v *Montefiore* (1866), an offer to buy shares in June had lapsed by November. If a time limit is specified, it must be complied with.

Knowledge check 21

What is an offer?

Invitations to treat

An invitation to treat is an invitation to someone to make an offer. It is important that you are able to distinguish between an offer and an invitation to treat. The significance of the distinction is that if an offer is made, all that is required from the other party is an acceptance. However, if there is an invitation to treat, the other party has to make an offer, which leaves the person who issued the invitation able to decide whether or not to accept the offer.

Whether something is an offer or an invitation depends on the circumstances. The following are invitations to treat:

- **Displays of goods in shop windows.** In *Fisher* v *Bell* (1961), a prosecution under the **Offensive Weapons Act 1959** failed because the offence was to offer for sale prohibited weapons. Although the shopkeeper was displaying a flick knife in his window with a price tag, the court decided that this amounted to an invitation to treat and not an offer for sale.
- **Goods on display in supermarkets and self-service stores.** This principle was established in Pharmaceutical Society of Great Britain v Boots (1953). Boots had opened a shop in which customers selected the products they wanted from displays and paid for them at a cash point. The court decided that the contract was made when the goods were presented at the cash desk and accepted by the cashier and not when they were taken from the shelves. The goods on display were an invitation to treat.
- **Small advertisements (e.g. in magazines or newspapers).** In *Partridge* v *Crittenden* (1968), an advertisement reading 'Bramblefinch cocks, bramblefinch

Examiner tip

Make sure you can distinguish between an offer and an invitation to treat as this is a common exam question.

Knowledge check 22

What is an invitation to treat?

hens, 25s each' was found to be an invitation, not an offer, so a prosecution for offering for sale a wild bird under the **Protection of Birds Act 1954** failed.
- **Price lists, catalogues etc.**
- **Responses to requests for information.** In *Harvey* v *Facey* (1893), Harvey telegraphed Facey and asked: 'Will you sell me Bumper Hall Pen? Telegraph lowest cash price.' Facey replied by telegram: 'Lowest cash price for Bumper Hall Pen £900.' Harvey sent a second telegram: 'We agree to buy Bumper Hall Pen at £900 asked by you.' It was held that Facey's telegram was not an offer but merely a statement of the price.
- **Auction sales.** In *British Car Auctions* v *Wright* (1972), a prosecution for offering to sell an unroadworthy car at auction failed, as putting goods into an auction is an invitation, not an offer for sale. The offer is made by the person making the bid.
- **Invitations to tender.** The person inviting the tenders is free to accept any of the tenders, and not necessarily the cheapest.

Acceptance

Knowledge check 23

What is acceptance?

Examiner tip

You may be asked a general question (e.g. one asking what acceptance is) or a more specific one (e.g. about the different ways in which acceptance can be communicated or about particular types of acceptance).

Examiner tip

You will almost certainly be asked to apply your understanding of offer/ acceptance. Often this will involve looking at the sequence of events and deciding whether a contract has been made. It is a good idea to draw up a timeline so that you can identify exactly what happened at each stage. This should then enable you to work out whether a valid contract has been made or whether for example the offer was revoked before it was accepted.

Acceptance is unqualified and unconditional agreement to all the terms of the offer by words or conduct. If conditions or qualifications are added, a counter-offer is created.
- **Acceptance must be communicated.** In *Felthouse* v *Bindley* (1862), the claimant offered to buy a horse from his nephew for £30 15s (£30.75), adding: 'If I hear no more about him, I shall consider the horse mine at £30 15s.' In the ensuing action, the court refused to regard the defendant's silence as assent, even though the nephew intended to accept the offer.
- **Acceptance can be inferred from conduct.** The principle seems to be that when you start to implement what is in the offer, you have accepted it.
- **If a method of acceptance is specified, it must be complied with.** However, in some circumstances another, equally good method might suffice (*Tinn* v *Hoffman*, 1873).
- **If no method is specified, any method will do, as long as it is effective.**
- **The 'postal rule' applies when the ordinary postal system is used.** Acceptance is valid when posted, even if the letter is lost in the post. Revocation is valid when received. In *Household Fire Insurance* v *Grant* (1879), a letter was lost in the post; nevertheless, there was a proper acceptance and a binding contract.
- **When instantaneous methods are used, acceptance is immediate as long as it is communicated.** Such methods include telephone, fax and e-mail, and acceptance is immediate as long as it gets through. In *Entores* v *Miles Far East* (1955), an English company in London was in communication by telex with a Dutch company in Amsterdam. The English company received an offer of goods from the Dutch company and made a counter-offer that the Dutch company accepted — all by telex. For purposes of jurisdiction, it was held that the contract was made in London, where the English company received the acceptance. Denning LJ suggested that the person receiving the acceptance will be bound even if he or she does not read the fax or telex until much later. However, in *Brinkibon* v *Stahag Stahl* (1983), a telex was received when the office was closed. It was held that the acceptance could become effective only when the office reopened.
- **A problem may arise when both parties use their own printed contract forms.** The Court of Appeal in *Butler Machine Tool* v *Ex-Cell-O Corporation* (1979)

applied the principle that when there is a 'battle of forms', a contract is made when the last of the forms is sent and received without objection.

Consideration

Consideration means that each side must promise to give or do something for the other. Consideration was defined in *Currie* v *Misa* (1875) as 'some right, interest, profit or benefit accruing to one party, or some forbearance, detriment, loss or responsibility given, suffered or undertaken by the other'. For example, if A promises to paint the house of B, the promise will only be enforceable as a contract if B has provided consideration. B's consideration in this situation would usually take the form of a payment of money or the promise of a future payment, but it could also consist of some other service (or future service) to which A might agree.

It is possible to have a valid contract even if one party does not provide consideration (e.g. if someone promises to make a gift), but only if the contract is made by deed.

Knowledge check 24

What is consideration?

The rules of consideration

Consideration is subject to the following rules:

- **Something of value must be given by both/all parties.** This basic principle distinguishes a contract from a purely gratuitous agreement (i.e. a promise to make a gift). The law says that consideration must be sufficient. This means that it must be real and tangible and have some actual value. In *White* v *Bluett* (1853), a promise not to complain about the contents of a will in return for the cancelling of a debt was considered to be intangible. It was not offering anything of real value or substance to the bargain.
- **It does not have to be adequate (i.e. the market price).** Where consideration is recognised by the law as having some value, it is described as 'real' or 'sufficient' consideration. Providing consideration has some value, the courts will not investigate its adequacy, nor will they investigate contracts to see if the parties have got equal value. In *Chappell and Co. Ltd* v *Nestlé Co. Ltd* (1960), Nestlé was running a special offer which involved people sending off three wrappers from Nestlé chocolate bars plus some money. It was held that the three wrappers were part of the consideration, even though on receipt the wrappers were thrown away.
- **It must not be past.** This means that any consideration must come after the agreement, rather than being something that has already been done. For example, if A paints B's house and then when the work is finished B promises to pay £100 for the work, this promise is unenforceable because A's consideration is past. In *Re McArdle* (1951), repairs were made to a property and afterwards people who were to inherit the property were asked to sign an agreement that they would reimburse the cost of the repairs. This agreement was not enforceable because the repairs had been done before the agreement was made.
- **It must not be an existing duty.** Doing something that you are already bound to do cannot amount to good consideration. The basic rule can be seen operating in *Stilk* v *Myrick* (1809), when two out of 11 sailors deserted a ship. The captain promised to pay the remaining crew extra money if they sailed the ship back, but later refused to pay. It was held that as the sailors were already bound by their contract to sail back and to meet such emergencies of the voyage, promising to

sail back was not valid consideration. Thus, the captain did not have to pay the extra money. However, in *Hartley* v *Ponsonby* (1857), when 19 out of 36 crew of a ship deserted, the captain promised to pay the remaining crew extra money to sail back, but later refused to pay saying that they were only doing their normal jobs. In this case, the ship was so seriously undermanned that the rest of the journey had become extremely hazardous. It was held that sailing the ship back in such dangerous conditions was over and above their normal duties. They were therefore entitled to the money. The modern example of *Williams* v *Roffey* (1991) seems to indicate that in business contracts the courts will try to find consideration in circumstances where, on the face of it, the consideration appears to be part of an existing duty. It was held by the Court of Appeal that where a party to an existing contract later agrees to pay an extra 'bonus' to ensure that the other party performs its obligations under the contract, that agreement is binding if the party agreeing to pay the bonus has thereby obtained some new practical advantage or avoided a disadvantage (in that case, the penalty clauses for late completion).

- **Third parties and consideration.** Some contracts involve an agreement to benefit someone other than the parties to the agreement. For example, in *Tweddle* v *Atkinson* (1861), an agreement was made between William Guy and John Tweddle that each would give a sum of money to William Tweddle, who had married William Guy's daughter. Unfortunately, William Guy died before making the payment and William Tweddle sued Guy's estate for the money. His claim failed. One of the judges based his decision on the fact that William Tweddle had offered no consideration, arguing that 'consideration must move from the promise' (i.e. the person to whom the promise is made). This case also raises the principle of **privity of contract**, which is the idea that only people who are a party to a contract can enforce it, even though it might intend to benefit third parties. The modern law, as set out in the **Contracts (Rights of Third Parties) Act 1999**, has significantly altered the position of third parties, allowing them to enforce agreements where they are expressly identified as beneficiaries, and it is likely that cases such as *Tweddle* v *Atkinson* would be decided differently now.

Examiner tip

You may be asked a general question (e.g. what is meant by consideration) or a more specific one (e.g. explaining what is meant by past consideration). You could also be asked to apply your understanding and decide whether good consideration has been offered in a particular scenario.

Knowledge check 25

In what kinds of agreements does the law presume that there is no intention to create legal relations?

Intention to create legal relations

In practice, it is quite easy for agreements to be made which contain offer and acceptance and in which both parties provide consideration. However, the law recognises that often the parties do not intend to create a legally binding contract. This is particularly the case within families and between friends. The law therefore says that there must be an intention to create legal relations, and it makes a distinction between **social and domestic agreements**, where the law assumes that there is no intention to create legal relations, and **commercial and business agreements**, where the law assumes that the parties intend the agreement to be legally binding.

Social and domestic agreements

Case law suggests that agreements within families will generally be treated as not legally binding. For example, in *Jones* v *Padavatton* (1969), Mrs Jones offered a monthly allowance to her daughter if she would give up her job in the USA and come to England and study to become a barrister. Because of accommodation problems, Mrs Jones bought a house in London where the daughter lived and received rents from other tenants. They later quarrelled and the mother sought repossession of the house. The court decided that there was no intention to create legal relations and that all the arrangements were just part of ordinary family life. Therefore, the mother was not liable on the maintenance agreement and could also claim the house.

In *Balfour* v *Balfour* (1919), the issue was the promise made by a husband to pay his wife an allowance while he was abroad. He failed to keep up the payments when their marriage broke down. The wife sued, but it was held that arrangements between husbands and wives are not contracts because the parties do not intend them to be legally binding. The court also decided that the wife had given no consideration for the husband's promise.

In contrast is the case of *Merrit* v *Merrit* (1970). The husband left his wife and they met to make arrangements for the future. The husband agreed to pay £40 per month maintenance, out of which the wife would pay the mortgage. When the mortgage was paid off, he would transfer the house from joint names into his wife's name. He wrote this down and signed the paper, but later refused to transfer the house. The court held that when the agreement was made, the husband and wife were no longer living together, so they must have intended the agreement to be binding, and their intention to base their future actions on the agreement was evidenced by the writing.

In cases that do not just involve members of the same family, the presumption that the arrangement is purely social will be rebutted if money has changed hands. In *Parker* v *Clarke* (1960), a young couple, the Parkers, were persuaded by an older couple to sell their house and move in with them. They would share the bills and the younger couple would inherit the house. Details of expenses were agreed and confirmation of the agreement was put in writing. It was held that the actions of the parties showed that they were serious and the agreement was intended to be legally binding.

Commercial and business agreements

An agreement made in a business context is presumed to be legally binding unless a different intent can be shown. In *Rose* v *Crompton Bros* (1925), a firm of paper manufacturers had entered into an agreement with the claimant to act as sole agents for the sale of the defendant's paper in the USA. The written agreement contained a clause that it was not entered into as a formal or legal agreement and would not be subject to legal jurisdiction in the courts, but was a record of the purpose and intention of the parties to which they honourably pledged themselves. It was held that the sole agency agreement was not binding owing to the inclusion of the 'honourable pledge clause'.

> **Knowledge check 26**
>
> What is the general rule about business contracts?

Football pools are a specific exception to the rule that agreements of a commercial nature are presumed to be legally binding. In *Jones* v *Vernon Pools* (1938) and in *Appleson* v *Littlewoods* (1939), the courts ruled that a statement on the coupon that the transaction was 'binding in honour only' meant that it was not legally binding.

On the other hand, situations where free gifts or prizes are promised are deemed to be legally binding, because the purpose is generally to promote the commercial interests of the body offering the gift or prize. In *McGowan* v *Radio Buxton* (2001), a prize in a radio competition was stated to be a Renault Clio car. However, when the prize was awarded it was a model car rather than a real one. The radio company claimed that there was no legally binding contract because it was not a commercial arrangement, but the court held that there was an intention to create legal relations and also that, looking at the transcript of the broadcast, people entering the competition would expect the prize to be a real car.

Summary

To be valid a contract must have:
- **offer** — the expression of a willingness to enter into a legally binding agreement:
  - can be made to individual or group
  - must be certain
  - can be made by any method to anyone
  - must be in existence when accepted
  - must be distinguished from invitation to treat
  - can be terminated by refusal/counter-offer/revocation/lapse of time
- **acceptance** — unqualified and unconditional acceptance of all terms in the offer:
  - must be communicated, though it can be inferred from conduct
  - must be by method specified or one as good as
  - if no method specified, can be by any method as long as it is effective
  - postal rule applies to acceptance using post
  - acceptance is immediate if instantaneous methods used
- **consideration:**
  - must have some value
  - must not be past
  - must not be existing duty
- **intention to create legal relations** — presumed in commercial and business agreements but not in social or domestic arrangements

Breach of contract

Knowledge check 27

What is breach of contract?

Knowledge check 28

What is anticipatory breach?

When a party fails to perform an obligation under a contract, it is said to be in breach of contract:
- **Actual breach** is when there is a failure to fulfil an obligation under the contract or to fulfil it to the required standard.
- **Anticipatory breach** occurs when one party shows by express words or by implications from his or her conduct at some time before performance is due that he or she does not intend to observe his or her obligations under the contract.

In cases of **anticipatory breach**, the innocent party is not under any obligation to wait until the date fixed for performance before commencing his or her action against the other party, but may immediately treat the contract as at an end and sue for damages. This principle was established in *Hochester* v *De La Tour* (1853), where an employer told his employee (a travelling courier) before the time for performance arrived that he would not require his services. The courier sued for damages at once. The court held that he was entitled to do so.

The injured party in an anticipatory breach of contract also has the option of waiting for the performance date to pass and then suing for breach. This is what happened in *Avery* v *Bowden* (1855), a case involving an agreement to supply cargo for a ship at a port in Russia. The claimant was advised that the cargo would not be supplied. At this stage, he could have sued successfully for anticipatory breach. Instead, he waited the 45 days until the date the cargo was due to be supplied and then sued.

Meanwhile, the Crimean War had broken out and performance of the contract became illegal. This illustrates the potential benefits of suing early in a case of anticipatory breach.

The rights of the injured party depend on the nature of the term broken:
- A **breach of warranty** is a breach of a minor term that does not go to the root of the contract and only gives rise to a claim for damages.
- A **breach of a condition** is a breach of an important term, giving the right to terminate the agreement and repudiate (cancel) the contract.

What this means in practice is that the injured party is prevented from using a minor breach of contract as an excuse for cancelling the whole contract. If, for example, a new car is delivered that has a faulty interior light, it is reasonable to expect the supplier to put it right at the supplier's expense (damages), but not reasonable to allow the purchaser to cancel the contract and demand his or her money back. If, on the other hand, there was a series of technical failures, which were not easy to put right and which resulted in the car breaking down, we can see that these relate to the very purpose of the contract and understand why the law, in this situation, might allow the purchaser to cancel the contract and buy a different car somewhere else.

Examiner tip
Be prepared for a general question on what breach of contract is and also for a question asking you the difference between actual and anticipatory breach. You can also expect to have to apply your understanding to a specific scenario and explain whether someone is in breach of contract.

Remedies for breach of contract

Repudiation of the contract

Repudiation is available only when there has been a breach of a condition. It is a far-reaching and drastic remedy and will result in any goods supplied or money paid under the contract being returned.

Damages

This remedy is available for all kinds of breach of contract, and may be appropriate even in cases where the contract has been rescinded. Damages may be classified as either liquidated or unliquidated:
- **Liquidated damages** are where the parties agree in advance what would be reasonable compensation in the event of a breach.
- **Unliquidated damages** are those which have not been agreed to in advance, and they will be determined by the court.

The purpose of damages

As stated in *Robinson* v *Harman* (1848), the principle is that 'when a party sustains loss by reason of a breach of contract he is, so far as money can do it, to be placed in the same situation with respect to damages as if the contract had been performed'.

Knowledge check 29

What is the purpose of damages?

Causation

There must be a causal link between the breach of contract and the damage suffered. This is a question of fact in each case. If the loss arises partly from the breach and partly as a result of intervening events, the party in breach may still be liable, providing the chain of causation has not been broken. For example, in *Stansbie* v *Troman* (1948), a decorator failed to lock the premises he had been working in and a thief entered and stole property. He was liable for the loss because it was the result of his failure to comply with his contractual duty to secure the premises on leaving.

In *Smith, Hogg and Co.* v *Black Sea Insurance Co.* (1940), a shipowner was held liable to a charterer in damages for loss of a cargo, which had been caused by a combination of perils of the sea and the unseaworthiness of the ship. However, in *The Monarch SS Co. Case* (1949), a shipowner was not liable to a charterer when, as a result of delay, the ship ran into a typhoon, because such an event could have occurred anywhere at any time.

Remoteness of damage

The courts have to decide how far the losses suffered by the injured party should be recoverable. The principle used is that losses are recoverable if they are reasonably within the contemplation of the parties as a probable result of the breach.

This principle is known as the rule in *Hadley* v *Baxendale* (1854). In that case, a new mill shaft was ordered and the carriers were late in delivering it, with the result that the whole mill was out of action for several days. The carriers said that they had not been told that the existing shaft was broken and therefore they did not know that their delay would result in the mill being unable to function. It was held that they were not liable for the loss of profit. The court judgement was that damages should be awarded only for losses that could fairly and reasonably be considered to have arisen naturally, in the usual course of things, or those that may be supposed to have been in the contemplation of the parties at the time they made the contract, as the probable result of it.

The application of the principle can be illustrated by the case of *Victoria Laundry* v *Newman Industries* (1949), in which a boiler was not delivered on time. Damages for the loss of profits from the laundry business were recoverable, but losses from not being able to take up a lucrative dyeing contract for the Ministry of Supply were not recoverable, because the defendant company had no knowledge of this contract and could not be expected to have had it in contemplation.

Mitigation

It is the duty of every party claiming damages to mitigate loss. This means that they need to ensure that as far as possible losses are kept to a minimum. There are three rules:

- The claimant cannot recover for loss that could have been avoided by taking reasonable steps.
- The claimant cannot recover for any loss that has actually been avoided, even if the claimant went further than was necessary in compliance with the above rule.
- The claimant may recover loss incurred in taking reasonable steps unsuccessfully to mitigate loss.

In *British Westinghouse* v *Underground Electric Railway of London* (1912), there was a contract for the supply of turbines, but those supplied were less efficient ones, which

Knowledge check 30

What kind of losses would be too remote and therefore not recoverable?

Knowledge check 31

What is mitigation of loss?

used more coal. The buyer accepted them and used them, before replacing them with turbines that were more efficient than those specified in the original contract. It was held that there was no duty to mitigate by buying new turbines, but since this had been done, the financial advantages gained from the new turbines had to be taken into account. Because the new turbines were so efficient, they more than covered the additional costs involved in replacing the original turbines, and so the buyer was not entitled to damages. However, if the buyer had claimed damages before buying the new turbines, it would have been successful.

However, a claimant is only expected to do what is reasonable; he or she would not be expected to 'take any step which a reasonable and prudent man would not ordinarily take in the course of his business'. For example, in *Pilkington* v *Wood* (1953), the claimant bought a house with defective title because of his solicitor's negligence. The solicitor argued that the claimant should have mitigated his loss by suing the vendor. The court held that 'the duty to mitigate does not go so far as to oblige the injured party to embark on a complicated and difficult piece of litigation against a third party...in order to protect his solicitor from the consequences of his own carelessness'.

Examiner tip

You are likely to be asked a question on how the court would calculate an award of damages. This will involve you explaining the purpose of damages and then explaining that a defendant will only be liable for losses that they have caused and which are reasonably foreseeable. Also the claimant is expected to mitigate their loss.

Summary

Breach of contract — failure to perform an obligation under the contract:
- breach of condition — breach of an important term — innocent party can repudiate the contract
- breach of warranty — breach of minor term — innocent party can only sue for damages
- actual breach
- anticipatory breach — innocent party does not have to wait for actual breach, but can treat contract as at an end and sue for damages

Damages is the remedy for all types of breach:
- Liquidated — where parties have agreed in advance what the damages should be in the event of a breach.
- Unliquidated — will be determined by the court.
- It must be clear that the breach of contract has caused the damage.
- Damages must not be too remote.
- The claimant has a duty to mitigate his/her loss.

Questions & Answers

How to use this section

This section provides 11 questions that cover most of the Unit 2 topics. All of the questions are followed by an A-grade answer, and some are also followed by a C/D-grade answer.

After attempting your own responses to the questions, you should study the specimen answers carefully — they provide an insight into the different techniques that these problem-solving questions require. Remember the importance of using cases effectively — failure to use cases is one of the most significant differences between A- and C/D-grade answers.

For problem-solving questions that are based on a short scenario, the mnemonic **IDEA** may help:

I   **Identify** the appropriate offence or tort element.

D   **Define** the specific offence or key element/rule of negligence.

E   **Explain** the various rules.

A   **Apply** the facts of the case to the rules explained, using **authorities** — both cases and statutes — to support your answers.

Examiner's comments

Each question is followed by a brief analysis of what to watch out for when answering it (shown by the icon ⊜). Each answer is accompanied by examiner's comments (preceded by the icon ⊜). These indicate where marks can be awarded and are intended to give you an insight into what examiners are looking for. For A-grade answers, these comments show why high marks would be given. The comments provided for C/D-grade answers point out the various weaknesses — lack of cases, inadequate explanation and irrelevant material, all of which cause marks to be lost.

To acquire the necessary skills and become more familiar with this style of examination question, it is a good idea to practise adapting the A-grade answers for different scenarios.

Examination technique

Case references

The importance of case references cannot be overemphasised. A 'case-free' answer rarely obtains more than a D or E grade, and will more often be awarded a U grade. Without appropriate case references, it is not possible to demonstrate a sound understanding of relevant law. Remember, the cases you have been taught do not just illustrate that rule of law; in many cases they *are* the law. Be aware that the mark scheme often prevents examiners awarding marks if there is no reference to case or statutory authorities. Even if the explanatory content of an answer could have merited a high mark, the absence of cases could mean losing 3–4 marks for a 8-mark question.

Matching cases to the correct legal rule

Many students appear to believe that as long as some cases are mentioned, it does not matter too much whether they are the right ones. Look carefully at the A- and C/D-grade answers in this section, and you will recognise the importance of using cases correctly. When revising, make a point of learning the correct case for each offence in terms of *actus reus* and *mens rea*, and for the separate rules in tort law.

Using cases

It is rarely necessary or desirable to describe the facts of the cases cited — the important part of a case is the legal rule it created or demonstrates. For example, a poor answer would cite the case of *Donoghue* v *Stevenson* and simply retell the story of Mrs Donoghue and the snail in the bottle. This is a waste of time; what the examiner wants to see is a short and accurate explanation of the 'neighbour principle'. It is a good idea to make a brief reference to the facts, such as mentioning that this is the 'snail in the bottle case', or the 'Jehovah's Witness case' (*R* v *Blaue*), or the 'cricket ball case' (*Bolton* v *Stone*). The only occasion when a more detailed description of the facts in a cited case is required is when the facts of the question scenario match them closely. A good example of this occurred in the June 2002 examination, when the tort scenario question was clearly based on the case of *Smith* v *Leech Brain*.

Omissions

Omitting details or explanations is the greatest single source of lost marks. Try to remember series of facts or rules, for example the three tests for duty of care and the different questions used to establish the 'reasonable man' test in breach of duty of care. In comparing the A- and C/D-grade answers in this section, make a note of the material that is omitted from the C/D-grade answers and try to spot the inadequate explanations.

AO3 marks

There are 2 marks for each AS paper section for quality of written communication. The easiest way to lose some of these is to misspell basic legal words such as *grievous*, *defendant*, *deterrence*, *assault* and *sentence*. Check your spelling, use paragraphs correctly and make your handwriting as clear as possible.

Planning your answer effectively

When you look at the A-grade answers, you will recognise immediately that there is a clear structure to each of them, usually demonstrated straight away by a simple, accurate and relevant first sentence. The C/D-grade answers lack this element of planning and structure. You should read the question carefully and make sure that you understand what it is asking, and then make a short plan — it could be in the form of a spider diagram or just a series of headings and subheadings. After this, read the question again to check that your plan is both relevant and accurate. Do not worry about how to introduce your answers — this is not an English exam. Look carefully at how the A-grade answers start and model your own technique on these.

Question 1 *Actus reus* and *mens rea*

(a) Explain what is meant by the term *'actus reus'*. (8 marks)

(e) The command 'explain' requires a full account of the key elements of *actus reus*, with effective use of case examples.

(b) Explain what is meant by the term *'mens rea'*. (8 marks)

(e) The command 'explain' requires a full account of the key elements of *mens rea*, with effective use of case examples.

(c) Explain the meaning of, and outline the reasons for, strict liability offences. (8 marks)

(e) This is a two-part question which requires a full description of the meaning of strict liability offences with effective use of case examples, followed by a brief explanation of the reasons why strict liability offences exist.

A-grade answer

(a) *Actus reus* is the physical element required for a criminal offence and in most cases it will be some form of positive action, but it also includes circumstances such as drink-driving or illegal drug possession. An *actus reus* could be both an act and circumstances, e.g. in criminal damage the offence consists of destroying/ damaging any property (the act) which belongs to another and for which act there is no lawful excuse (the circumstances). The *actus reus* must be a voluntary act, i.e. the act/omission must have occurred because of a conscious exercise of will of the defendant. In *Hill* v *Baxter*, the judge provided a hypothetical example of a driver who lost control of his car when attacked by a swarm of bees, and stated that in such a case, there would be no criminal liability. Each separate crime has its own specific *actus reus,* e.g. for battery it is the infliction of unlawful personal violence.

In most cases, the *actus reus* will be a positive act but there are circumstances where it can be an omission — a failure to act where the law imposes a duty to act. Examples include *R* v *Pittwood* where the level-crossing keeper failed to close the railway gate to vehicles and a man was killed. Here, it was held that his duty arose from his employment contract. Another case is *R* v *Stone and Dobinson.* Here a couple who lived together invited Stone's middle-aged sister who was anorexic to come and live with them. Although Stone and Dobinson were aware that the woman was totally neglecting herself and was rapidly deteriorating they did nothing to assist her. After she died, they were convicted of her manslaughter — they had assumed a duty of care for her, a duty which they could easily have discharged by calling for help or by providing even basic care.

(e) **8/8 marks awarded.** This is a sound answer which gives a full explanation of *actus reus* and makes effective use of cases, especially to illustrate omissions.

(b) *Mens rea* is defined as the mental element required for criminal liability. It comprises the following — intention and recklessness. Intention is either direct which means it was the aim, purpose or objective of the defendant to achieve a particular result *(R v Mohan)* or oblique. This occurs where the defendant has undoubtedly brought about the end result, e.g. unlawful killing but has done so in circumstances where he argues that he neither desired nor foresaw that particular result. Such an argument requires the linked issues of (objective) probability and (subjective) foreseeability to be considered. After considerable judicial debate, it is now settled law that for a jury to return a guilty verdict in a murder case where oblique intent is the issue, they must be satisfied that the defendant foresaw death or at least GBH as being virtually certain, barring unforeseeable intervention — *R v Nedrick/Woollin*. In *R v Matthews and Alleyne*, it was confirmed that this is an evidential test. Recklessness now is only subjective, following the House of Lords decision in *R v G*. This requires the prosecution to prove that the defendant took an unjustifiable risk while recognising that his action could result in property damage or personal injury. The leading case is that of *R v Cunningham* where the defendant's conviction was quashed as there was no evidence that he realised that when he broke into a gas meter, he had caused gas to escape, and that this could cause injury to anyone in the house.

ⓔ **8/8 marks awarded.** This response answers the question fully — all elements are well explained, especially oblique intent. All relevant cases are included. Note that the case facts are only used in *Cunningham*. Describing the facts of leading cases will always earn marks, but it is not always essential.

(c) Strict liability offences are no fault offences where the prosecution is not obliged to prove *mens rea*. These offences are often referred to as regulatory or quasi-criminal offences as they do not usually result in the stigma of a criminal conviction. Most penalties for these offences are fines, although in *Gammon v Attorney-General of Hong Kong*, the fact that the offence was punishable with a fine of HK$250,000 and up to 3 years' imprisonment was not inconsistent with the imposition of strict liability. A good example of such a crime occurred in *Callow v Tillstone*, where the defendant, who was a butcher, asked a vet to examine a carcass to ensure it was fit for human consumption. On receiving the vet's assurance that it was fit, the butcher offered it for sale. However, the vet had been negligent and the meat was contaminated. The defendant was convicted of exposing unsound meat for sale, even though he had exercised due care.

Another important case is that of *Sweet v Parsley* where the defendant's conviction for 'managing premises used for illegal drug use' was quashed by the House of Lords. It was argued that the offence was a serious one which could have resulted in a custodial sentence being imposed, and as the Act had not clearly defined the offence as one of strict liability, *mens rea* required to be proved. Further illustrative cases which confirm the offence was one of strict liability are *Alphacell v Woodward* (environmental pollution) and *Shah v Harrow LBC* (selling lottery tickets to a minor child).

ⓔ This paragraph fully addresses the first part of the question — both *Callow* v *Tilstone* and *Sweet* v *Parsley* are accurately described. The additional cases referred to confirm this is a sound response.

> Most of these are created by statute for the protection of society — many road traffic offences are strict liability as are offences to protect consumers (e.g. dangerous goods regulations) and workers in factories and mines (e.g. safety regulations). Another reason for having such offences is that it is much easier and quicker to prosecute these in court. A further reason for having strict liability is that it acts as a deterrent to companies to ensure higher safety standards.

ⓔ **8/8 marks awarded.** As required by the question, this section is much shorter as it only needed to outline the reasons, yet it is still a sound answer.

Question 2 **Coincidence of *actus reus* and *mens rea***

Explain the legal rule which states that for a crime to be committed the *actus reus* and *mens rea* must coincide.

(5 marks)

ⓔ The command word 'explain' requires a full explanation with effective use of case authorities.

A-grade answer

This means that the *mens rea* must occur at the same time as the *actus reus*. It is a major requirement for the imposition of criminal liability that the prosecution proves both the necessary *actus reus* and *mens rea*, but it must further be proved that these two elements coincided.

In most instances, this rule does not create problems, for example the attacker who strikes his victim with a broken glass or the murderer who kills his victim by shooting her with a shotgun, but there have been several real cases where this issue has been the central legal question which has to be resolved in order for the defendant to be convicted.

The leading case example is that of *Thabo Meli* v *R*, where the appellants attacked their victim intending to kill him; wrongly believing that the victim was dead, they pushed his body over a cliff to dispose of it. Medical evidence confirmed that the victim in fact died some hours later of exposure. The Judicial Committee of the Privy Council considered the defence argument that while the initial attack was accompanied by *mens rea*, that was not the actual cause of death, while the second act which was the cause of death was not accompanied by *mens rea*. However, in dismissing that argument, it was held here that 'it was impossible to divide up what was really one transaction'. The appellants' murder conviction was upheld.

This approach of 'continuing act' or 'linked transactions' was upheld in the manslaughter cases of *R* v *Church* and *R* v *Le Brun*. A final case example is that of *Fagan* v *Metropolitan Police Commissioner*.

In conclusion, from the above cases it can be seen that in the few instances where it has been argued as a defence that the *actus reus* and *mens rea* do not coincide, the courts have taken a robust and realistic line that, provided there is a 'linked transaction' or 'continuing act', it does not matter if the *actus reus* and *mens rea* do not 'precisely' coincide.

ⓔ **5/5 marks awarded.** This is a comprehensive and well-argued answer. There is a clear introduction, which immediately establishes what this rule means. The student then takes one of the best illustrative cases and provides a sound factual explanation from which the legal rule can easily be ascertained. Further cases confirm the student's detailed understanding of the 'continuing act' theory. This is confirmed again by a sound concluding paragraph.

C/D-grade answer

If the *actus reus* and the *mens reus* don't coincide, then the charge can be dropped altogether. The *actus reus* can usually be proved quite easily but the *mens reus* is more difficult because it means 'getting into the mind' of the offender, and trying to find out why he or she committed the offence. In a case called *Thabo Meli* gang beat up a victim intending to kill him, and they threw him over a cliff. The victim later died from exposure. Therefore, the defence argued that the men were not guilty as they did not have the *mens rea* when they threw him over the cliff, only during the beating. However, the judge found them to be guilty of murder, using what is known as the 'continuing act' theory.

ⓔ **2 or 3/5 marks awarded.** This is a weak answer; the student gives a confused account of this rule from the beginning. Reference to how *actus reus* and *mens rea* can be proved is entirely irrelevant (and incorrect). Some marks are given for the case reference, where the facts are explained with reasonable accuracy and the 'continuing act' rule is identified, but not properly described.

Question 3 **Non-fatal offences (I)**

When John is drinking with friends in a pub, some youths start fighting among themselves. John approaches them and tries to stop them fighting. Dave, one of the gang, shouts at John: 'Mind your own business — if you want to interfere, I'll thump you.' Dave then lashes out at John and punches him twice in the face, causing serious bruising and a black eye.

Discuss the possible criminal liability of Dave with respect to the above incident.

(8 marks)

ⓔ You need to identify and explain the various offences which Dave may have committed in the scenario.

A-grade answer

When Dave shouted at John, he could be guilty of assault defined in s.39 of the Criminal Justice Act 1988 as 'intentionally or recklessly causing the victim to apprehend immediate unlawful violence.' In *R* v *Constanza*, it was held that words alone could constitute assault, provided John believed he was about to be attacked, although here the threat was conditional on John continuing to 'interfere'. Dave's shout was clearly intentional. Dave's action of lashing out at John would also constitute the *actus reus* of assault.

ⓔ This provides a clear definition of assault in terms of both *actus reus* and *mens rea*. The use of the relevant case is effective, as is the recognition that the threat by Dave was conditional.

Once Dave lashed out at John, he committed a battery and as it caused serious bruising and a black eye, he could be charged under s.47 of the Offences against the Person Act 1861 of assault (here battery) occasioning actual bodily harm (ABH). A battery consists of intention or reckless infliction of violence on the victim which was hostile as occurred here. There is no issue with either the *actus reus* or *mens rea* of battery. The *mens rea* of intent is obviously established. ABH was described in *R* v *Miller* as 'any hurt or injury calculated to interfere with the comfort or health of the victim, provided it is more than transient or trifling'. The serious bruising and black eye would meet this definition. The *mens rea* for s.47 is the same as battery — this was confirmed by *R* v *Savage* where it was held that for a s.47 conviction, the Crown does not need to prove that the defendant intended or was reckless as to inflicting ABH. All that is required is proof that the defendant intended or was reckless as to committing the offence of assault or battery — here it would be battery, which has been described above.

ⓔ **8/8 marks awarded.** This is a sound answer. It clearly explains the offence of s.47 ABH as a battery which causes ABH. Both *actus reus* and *mens rea* are accurately described and applied.

C-grade answer

According to the scenario, Dave shouted at John and then struck him twice, which resulted in bruising and a black eye. I think that Dave could be charged with both assault and battery, which are common-law offences. Assault is defined as intentionally or recklessly causing the victim to believe he or she is going to be attacked — here, by shouting at John, Dave could have caused John to think that he was about to be struck. It could also be assault, of course, if John saw the blows coming. Because Dave threw the punches deliberately, the *mens rea* of intention is present.

In the case of battery, this offence is committed when the defendant strikes the victim — there is no need for any level of injury to be inflicted. Here both the bruising and the black eye would be sufficient for the *actus reus* of battery.

The *mens rea* of battery is either intention to strike the victim or recklessness — in non-fatal offences recklessness is 'Cunningham' or subjective recklessness, which means that the defendant must have recognised that he or she was taking a risk.

@ **5/8 marks awarded.** Although both assault and battery are reasonably defined and explained, there is no reference to s.47 ABH which by itself would restrict this answer to a maximum of 5 marks. As a general rule, if there are minor injuries such as occurred here, s.47 ABH should be considered. Another weakness is the very limited use of case law.

Question 4 **Non-fatal offences (2)**

Richard and his girlfriend Alison had a serious argument, at the end of which Alison, in her rage, picked up a kitchen knife and threw it at Richard. It struck him in the shoulder and caused a bad cut and damaged tendons.

Discuss the possible criminal liability of Alison with respect to the incident with the kitchen knife. (8 marks)

ⓔ As in question 3, the command words — 'discuss the possible criminal liability' — require you to identify and explain the various offences which Alison may have committed in the scenario.

A-grade answer

Given the cut to the shoulder and the damaged tendons, Alison would be liable to be charged under s.20 of the Offences Against the Person Act 1861. This offence is malicious wounding and/or inflicting grievous bodily harm (GBH).

The *actus reus* comprises wounding, which is defined in *C (a minor)* v *Eisenhower* as a breach in the inner and outer layers of the skin, or grievous bodily harm, which was described in *R* v *Saunders* as 'serious harm'. The cut to Richard's shoulder would certainly qualify as a wound, and damaged tendons could be regarded as sufficiently serious to be GBH. Both injuries would require prompt hospital treatment.

The *mens rea* of s.20 is intention or recklessness as to causing some harm, not necessarily wounding or GBH. This was laid down in the case of *R* v *Mowatt* and confirmed in *R* v *Grimshaw*. Recklessness here is 'Cunningham' or subjective recklessness — conscious taking of an unjustified risk.

While Alison may deny having intended to cause such injuries, her conduct was certainly reckless when she threw a kitchen knife at Richard. The prosecution would argue that when Alison picked up and then threw the knife at Richard, she would have realised she was taking an unjustified risk of causing some harm at least, even if she were to argue that she did not intend to cause any injury.

Because the *actus reus* of the more serious offence — s.18 wounding or causing GBH with intent — is identical to that of s.20, it is possible for Alison to be charged with this offence. The only difference between the two offences is in the issue of *mens rea*. Section 18 is a specific intent offence — the prosecution must prove that the defendant intended to cause GBH. As Alison used a weapon, this would be easier to prove. Intent here could be either direct intent or oblique intent, whereby the jury would have to believe that Alison foresaw serious injury as being 'virtually certain' in order to convict her under s.18.

ⓔ **8/8 marks awarded.** In such cases where there are clearly injuries consistent with ss.20 and 18, it can be difficult to know whether to start with s.20 or s.18, especially where, as here, a weapon was used. Provided both offences are considered, and *actus reus* and *mens rea* elements are explained and then applied, it does not usually matter which offence is dealt with first.

Definitions of wounding and GBH are clearly stated with the use of relevant cases, as is the correct definition of the *mens rea* of s.20 with good application. The alternative offence of s.18 is defined and, because it is a specific intent offence, both direct and oblique intent are discussed.

C/D-grade answer

In this case, Alison could be charged with a number of offences according to the harm caused to the victim, Richard. As a result of Alison's actions, Richard has suffered a bad cut and damaged tendons. Alison could be charged with ABH s.47 or even s.20 GBH under the Offences against the Person Act 1861.

Section 47 ABH is an assault which causes ABH and Richard's injuries could be ABH. The *mens rea* is intention or recklessness and Alison intended to throw the knife at him.

ⓔ This is a much weaker and more confused introduction — the failure to recognise the injuries are too serious for s.47 ABH is a major error. This weakness is then compounded by the failure to explain the correct *actus reus* and *mens rea* for s.47: you should *never* state that the *mens rea* is intention or recklessness — these terms must be directed at a particular result, e.g. for s.47 that is intent or recklessness as to the offence of assault or battery.

Since the injuries are quite serious, Alison could also be charged with s.20 GBH or wounding. GBH is simply defined as serious harm (Saunders) and wounding means blood flowed. Again the *mens rea* is intent or recklessness and Alison deliberately threw the knife at Richard.

ⓔ **4 or 5/8 marks awarded.** Significant weaknesses continue in discussing s.20 where again, *mens rea* is incorrectly stated. There is no consideration of a possible s.18 charge, and the final problem is the almost complete absence of case references.

Question 5 **Sentencing**

Using the scenario in question 3 about Dave and John, and assuming that Dave were to be convicted, outline the aims of sentence that a judge would consider and explain the range of sentences that would be available to the judge.

(8 marks)

ⓔ This is a two-part question. The first part requires an outline of aims — this should be a brief explanation of at least three separate aims. The second part has the command word 'explain' which calls for a fuller account. You should also provide a brief conclusion suggesting a suitable sentence.

A-grade answer

There are five main aims of sentencing:

- Retribution means that a person who has broken the rules shall be punished. It also includes the idea of 'just deserts'.
- Deterrence is another aim. Individual deterrence aims to prevent the offender from reoffending, while general deterrence aims to deter others.
- Rehabilitation aims to reform, treat or cure the 'criminal deviance' which 'caused' the criminal to offend. Such an aim results in greater resources being used to provide good educational and counselling services in prison.
- Protection of society requires that serious (especially violent) offenders should be imprisoned: the 'prison works' idea. Under s.227 of the Criminal Justice Act 2003, extended sentences are possible, which allow an extra period of custody where there is a significant risk of serious harm to the public.
- Reparation pays attention to the needs and views of victims, and ensures that the offender 'puts right' the damage he or she has done.

There are a number of sentences that a court could impose on Dave:

- Custodial sentences involve a term of imprisonment. This may be immediate or suspended, when the prison sentence is not activated unless the defendant commits further offences.
- Community sentences are also possible. The Criminal Justice Act 2003 created one community order under which any requirements can be included that the court considers necessary. They can include all the previous community sentences, such as community punishment orders, where the offender has to perform a set number of hours of unpaid work, from 40 to 240 hours over a 12-month period, and community rehabilitation orders, which place the offender under the supervision of a probation officer, and also some new requirements, such as a curfew requirement or an alcohol treatment requirement. Each order should reflect the seriousness of the offence.
- There are also financial sentences, which are fines and can be enforced through an attachment of earnings order. Compensation orders can be made for injuries caused or property damaged.

- Discharges may be absolute or conditional, the latter meaning that if the offender commits a further offence in the stated period, then the original offence may be resentenced.

The maximum sentence for battery is 6 months; for s.47 ABH it is 5 years. If Dave was convicted of assault and s.47 ABH, the judge would consider a retributive and possibly individual deterrent sentence, and would be likely to impose a community order or a short custodial sentence.

8/8 marks awarded. This is a comprehensive answer. Both aspects of the question — aims and types of sentence — are explained clearly and accurately, with appropriate use of statutory authority. Finally, the maximum sentences for each offence are stated correctly.

C/D-grade answer

If Dave were to be convicted of an offence, the courts might use a number of sentences available. One type of sentence would be a suspended sentence, which means that if he reoffends within a given time, the original offence will be brought up again. He could also get probation or a community service order.

The most common type of sentence is a fine, but I think for Dave's offence this would not be sufficiently severe, and I would impose a prison sentence — this would deter him from reoffending and while in prison he could receive some form of counselling about alcohol.

4/8 marks awarded. This is not a well-focused answer and it has limited factual content. The student has made the common mistake of trying to answer the question with regard to the specific offender mentioned in the scenario, instead of answering it as a general sentencing question. The issue of 'aims' is dealt with only in passing in terms of the deterrent effect of a prison sentence and the implied rehabilitative effect of alcohol counselling.

Question 6 **Negligence (I)**

(a) Explain how a court decides whether a duty of care is owed in negligence.   (8 marks)

ⓔ The command 'explain' requires a full account of the key elements of duty of care, with effective use of case examples.

(b) Explain what is meant by breach of duty of care.   (8 marks)

ⓔ The command 'explain' requires a full account of the key elements of breach of duty with effective use of case examples.

(c) Explain the rules of factual causation and remoteness of damage.   (8 marks)

ⓔ The command 'explain' requires a full account of the key elements of both factual causation and remoteness of damage, with effective use of case examples.

A-grade answer

(a) The issue of whether a duty of care is owed by a defendant is determined by using the 'neighbour test' from *Donoghue* v *Stevenson* where Lord Atkin held that 'one must take reasonable care to avoid acts or omissions which you can reasonably foresee would be likely to injure your neighbour'. In *Caparo Industries plc* v *Dickman* the incremental test laid down these questions:
- Was damage or harm foreseeable?
- Is there sufficient proximity (close relationship) between the wrongdoer and the victim?
- Is it just and reasonable to impose a duty of care?

The test of foreseeability requires that a reasonable person would have foreseen some damage or harm being caused to the victim if the defendant did not take reasonable care — it is an objective test. A good example of this is the case of *Kent* v *Griffiths* where a doctor summoned an ambulance to take a patient urgently to hospital. The ambulance failed to arrive within a reasonable time and the patient suffered a heart attack which would not have occurred had the ambulance arrived in time. It was held it was reasonably foreseeable that the claimant would suffer some harm as a result of the late arrival of the ambulance.

The proximity test means that the claimant and the defendant have to be close to each other at the time of the negligence, in terms of time, space or relationship. In many cases, the proximity test and the foreseeability test are the same. In *Bourhill* v *Young*, it was decided that the motorcyclist did not owe a duty of care to Mrs Bourhill who at the time of the crash was standing behind a solid barrier and not within his field of vision, and was in no way at risk from his speed and therefore there was not sufficient proximity between the claimant and defendant.

The final question — is it just and reasonable to impose a duty of care — relates to the issue of policy. This question has arisen in the following contexts — nervous shock, pure economic loss and statutory duties where judges have taken on board the difficulties which might be caused were there no rules to limit potential liability. Judges use this test to prevent the 'floodgates opening'; that is to stop the case leading to courts being swamped by many other cases. In *Mulcahy* v *MoD*, the courts used his test to stop a soldier on active duty receiving compensation for an injury as it would not be to fair impose a duty of care on the MoD in battlefield situations.

ⓔ 8/8 marks awarded. This answer comprehensively covers all the rules on duty — the brief opening reference to *Donoghue* v *Stevenson* and the 'neighbour test' is still relevant. Note how well the cases are used to explain how each rule 'works'.

(b) The test used by courts to decide whether the defendant has breached his or her duty of care is 'the reasonable man' test, whereby the defendant is judged by the standard of the reasonable person. In *Blythe* v *Birmingham Waterworks*, Alderson LJ defined breach of duty as 'doing something which a reasonable person would not do, or failing to do something which the reasonable person would have done'. The test is an objective one which does not take into account any characteristics of the actual defendant — this was shown in *Nettleship* v *Weston* where the learner driver defendant was judged by the standard of a reasonably competent motorist. For professional people, the *Bolam* test is used where the defendant has to prove that he/she has the level of competence usually to be expected of an ordinary skilled member of that profession. Children are judged against the 'reasonable child' who is the same age as the defendant — *Mullins* v *Richard*.

Several risk factors are then considered by the judge such as the probability of harm, magnitude of risk and the cost of taking precautions. In *Bolton* v *Stone*, it was held that because the risk of harm was so low and the cricket club had taken sufficient precautions, there was no breach. However, in *Paris* v *Stepney LBC*, the defendant who had failed to provide goggles to a one-eyed employee was held liable because of the additional vulnerability of the employee. In *Latimer* v *AEC Ltd*, it was decided that since the defendant had taken reasonable precautions by spreading sawdust on his factory floor, he was not in breach of duty as the only other precaution he could have taken would be to have closed his factory altogether and that was disproportionate to the level of risk.

ⓔ 8/8 marks awarded. This is a sound answer with a particularly strong opening paragraph which deals with all aspects of the 'reasonable man' test. The answer then continues with a brief account — well supported by cases — of the key risk factor tests.

(c) The factual rule of causation is the 'but for' rule which simply asks whether 'but for' the breach of duty by the defendant, the damage/harm to the claimant would have occurred. The leading case example is *Barnett* v *Chelsea and Kensington HMC* where the doctor was clearly in breach of duty when he failed to examine a seriously ill patient and sent him home and the patient died later that evening. However, because the patient was suffering from acute arsenic poisoning, it was held that his death was inevitable and the doctor's poor treatment was not the cause of death.

Remoteness of damage is a measure of the foreseeability of the damage arising from the breach of duty. A defendant will only be liable for damage that was reasonably foreseeable by the defendant at the time of the breach of duty. This rule was laid down in the *Wagon Mound (No. 1)* case where a ship had negligently discharged oil into Sydney harbour. The slick spread to the claimant's wharf where welding was taking place. Although the claimants were advised there was no risk of the oil catching fire, it did and damage was caused to two ships. It was decided that this damage was too remote from the discharge of the oil, and the defendants were only liable for the fouling caused to the wharf.

Another rule is that if the kind of damage is reasonably foreseeable, it does not matter if it occurred in an unforeseeable way. In *Hughes* v *Lord-Advocate*, the claimant was badly burned when a paraffin lamp exploded — it was held that as burns were foreseeable, the defendant was liable even though the explosion itself was not foreseeable. Finally, the 'thin skull' rule may be applied — take your victim as you find him. In *Smith* v *Leech Brain*, the defendant was held liable for the cancer which was started when a molten piece of metal burned the claimant's lip.

ⓔ 8/8 marks awarded. This is another sound answer — again, note how fully the facts of the key cases (*Barnett* and the *Wagon Mound*) are explained. The additional (albeit brief) notes on the *Hughes* and *Smith* cases confirm this is a sound answer.

Question 7 **Negligence (2)**

Fred is driving his car along a busy high street when his mobile phone rings. While reaching out for his phone, he loses control of the car and crashes into a lamp post. His passenger, Kate, suffers severe whiplash injuries. These injuries lead to a rare condition affecting the central nervous system, which causes Kate to experience partial paralysis to her left side.

Discuss whether, in the above scenario, Fred has been negligent towards Kate. (8 marks)

A-grade answer

Kate would first need to prove that Fred owed her a duty of care, using the Caparo tests. The first of these is reasonable foreseeability; it could be argued that it is entirely foreseeable that if a driver is distracted, the car could crash and a passenger could be injured. As Kate was a passenger in Fred's car, there is clearly proximity in terms of time and space. As road traffic accidents constitute a common 'duty' situation and no policy issues are involved, it seems likely that it will be decided that Fred owed Kate a duty of care.

As regards breach, Kate has to prove that Fred did not behave as a reasonable driver would have. This test is objective (*Nettleship* v *Weston*), and in deciding this, various risk factors are considered. The first of these is probability of harm. It could be argued there was a high degree of probability that, having picked up the phone and being distracted, Fred could lose control of the car and it would crash. The magnitude of probable harm is high in any car accident. Finally, Fred could easily have taken appropriate precautions to avoid the harm by not answering the phone, which the reasonable and prudent driver would have done.

Damage is easily proved under the 'but for' rule, and the whiplash injuries suffered by Kate are certainly not too remote a consequence as they are reasonably foreseeable. As for the partial paralysis, this would be dealt with using the 'thin skull' rule, which requires defendants to take their victims as they find them. The leading case here is *Smith* v *Leech Brain*, where the defendant was held liable for the death of the victim from cancer, which was caused by the negligent spillage of molten metal.

Therefore, it is likely that Fred will be held liable in negligence towards Kate for all her injuries.

@ **8/8 marks awarded.** This is a strong and clearly structured answer that deals effectively with all the relevant rules on duty, breach and damage. In all cases, there is sufficient explanation and application of the rules.

C-grade answer

It could be argued that it is foreseeable that if a driver answers a mobile phone, he or she could lose control of the car and crash, and obviously there is no problem with proximity. For breach, there was a high probability that harm could be caused to a passenger in a crash, and that the harm could be serious. Finally, it is clear that the breach was the factual 'but for' cause of Kate's injuries and was not too remote.

ⓔ **4 or 5/8 marks awarded.** The contrast with the A-grade answer is stark; this answer has not explained why 'there is no problem with proximity', and there is no reference to the policy test. On breach, there is no reference to the 'reasonable man' test or to the cost of precautions. On damage, the issue of Kate's partial paralysis is ignored, so there is no mention of the 'thin skull' rule. Application is also much weaker — the answer is virtually just a series of unargued assertions.

Question 8 **Damages**

Look again at the scenario outlined in question 7. If Kate proved all the elements of the tort of negligence, she would be entitled to damages. Describe the methods used by the courts to assess the amount of damages to be awarded.

(8 marks)

(e) Although the claimant, Kate, is mentioned in this question, it is in fact a straightforward 'explanation' question with no application required. As such, it requires a full description of both special and general heads of damage. In questions on damages, use of case law is not really important.

A-grade answer

The purpose of damages is, as far as money can do this, to put the claimant in the position he or she was in before the tortious act.

(e) This is a good way to begin an answer on damages — explain their purpose.

For purposes of calculating the award, damages are divided into two kinds — special and general damages.

Special damages comprise quantifiable financial losses up to the date of trial and are assessed separately from other awards because the exact amount to be claimed is known at the time of the trial. They include:

- loss of earnings from date of tort to trial
- medical expenses — any services or treatment; only such expenses as are considered reasonable by the court are recoverable
- expenses to cover special facilities, such as the cost of special living accommodation — the measure of damages here will be the sum spent to obtain the special facility and its running costs

General damages is a term that covers all losses that are not capable of exact quantification, and they are divided into pecuniary and non-pecuniary damages. The major head of pecuniary damages is that of future loss of earnings. This is calculated using the notions of multiplicand — a sum to represent the claimant's annual net lost earnings — and multiplier — a notional figure which represents a number of years by which the multiplicand is to be multiplied in order to calculate the future losses. Any social security benefits etc. will be deducted from the damages award.

- Other future losses: the claimant is entitled to an award to cover the cost of future care — nursing requirements, physiotherapy etc.
- Non-pecuniary losses: these include pain and suffering. Compensation for these is subjective as they are impossible to measure in terms of money.
- Loss of amenity: the claimant is entitled to damages for the inability to enjoy life in various ways, in particular impairment of the senses — this will include, for example, inability to run or walk, to play sport or play a musical instrument.
- Damages for the injury itself: injuries are itemised and particular sums are awarded for these on the basis of precedents.

ⓔ **8/8 marks awarded.** Note how this answer is laid out. It is structured clearly into the main sections or headings. This type of question, where a number of separate points are required, lends itself to this 'report-writing' answer style. This is a comprehensive and accurate answer, covering all the main points of damages. Note also that there is no attempt to quantify the actual amount of damages that Kate might receive — indeed, Kate does not feature at all in this answer. Remember that quantification of the amount of damages is not included in this unit — only the types or heads of damages.

C-grade answer

In deciding the amount of damages Kate would receive, the court would have to consider the type of damages she should receive. She may claim both special and general damages — special damages are those which can be costed up to the time of trial, such as medical expenses. General damages are more difficult to deal with — the most important of these is future loss of earnings. Kate's injuries, especially the paralysis, might lead to her being unemployed for a considerable period of time, maybe even permanently, and so the judge will have to decide on a very large amount of money to compensate Kate.

Other types of damages include compensation for the injury itself — here, because Kate now suffers from paralysis, which is a serious condition, she would be awarded a great deal of compensation. Finally, she could receive money in respect of loss of amenity.

ⓔ **5/8 marks awarded.** This answer has little structure to it when compared to the A-grade answer above. There is some knowledge of the various types of damages, but these are not explained adequately. The student makes the serious error of trying to personalise the answer as regards the claimant in the scenario, Kate.

Question 9 Contract: offer

Explain what is meant by the term 'offer' in contract law. (8 marks)

(e) 'Explain' is asking you to give the meaning of the term, but for 8 marks you have to provide more than a simple definition.

A-grade answer

An offer could be defined as an expression of willingness to contract on certain terms, made with the intention that it will become binding on acceptance. It can be specific — made to one person or group of people — or general and not limited in who it is directed at as in *Carlill* v *Carbolic Smoke Ball Co.*

An offer may be made by any method. It can be made in writing, verbally or by conduct (e.g. by picking an item up and taking it to the cash desk).

It must be distinguished from an invitation to treat, which is where someone is invited to make an offer. Goods on display in shops (*Fisher* v *Bell*) or supermarkets (*Boots* v *Pharmaceutical Co.*) are invitations, as are most advertisements (*Partridge* v *Crittenden*).

An offer must be certain, which means that its terms must be clear and definite without any ambiguity. For example, in *Guthing* v *Lynn* a promise to pay an extra £5 'if the horse is lucky' was considered too vague to constitute an offer.

Another rule is that an offer must be communicated. A person cannot accept what he or she does not know about and the offer must still be in existence when it is accepted.

An offer can be brought to an end at any point before acceptance. It can be ended in a number of different ways. A refusal will end an offer, and the case of *Hyde* v *Wrench* illustrates the fact that a counter-offer will also terminate an offer.

An offer can be revoked (withdrawn) at any time, but this must be before acceptance. The revocation must be received before the acceptance is made (e.g. *Byrne* v *Van Tienhoven*).

(e) **8/8 marks awarded.** This question requires description. This response clearly outlines the main elements of an offer and goes further than a simple definition. A variety of cases is used to illustrate how the rules work.

C-grade answer

An offer is when someone indicates that he or she would be willing to enter into a binding agreement. It could be made to the whole world as in the famous *Carbolic Smoke Ball* case.

An offer may be made by any method, including through conduct as when picking up an item and taking it to the cash desk. It must be distinguished from an invitation to treat.

An offer can be ended in a number of different ways. A refusal will end an offer and so will a counter-offer. This is what happened in *Hyde* v *Wrench*.

e **5/8 marks awarded.** This answer makes a number of points and refers to two cases. However, it is too brief and omits a lot of relevant information, such as the definition of an invitation to treat or an explanation of how it is distinguished from an offer. The section on the ending of offers is also underdeveloped and could have been improved by explaining what is meant by a counter-offer.

Question 10 Contract: offer and acceptance

Gary offers to sell his car to Sandeep for £2,000. Sandeep offers £1,500 and Gary says that he will accept nothing less than £2,000. Sandeep goes away to think about it. She returns the following week to say that she will pay £2,000. Meanwhile, Gary has sold the car to someone else.

Applying the rules on offer and acceptance, advise Sandeep of her rights.   (8 marks)

ⓔ This question requires application. This means that the rules have to be explained and then applied to the facts. Note that sometimes you are asked to explain the rules in one question and then apply them in a later question.

A-grade answer

An offer is an expression of willingness to contract on certain terms and an acceptance is unqualified and unconditional agreement to all of those terms. An offer will come to an end if it is rejected, if there is a counter-offer, if there is revocation and sometimes if there is lapse of time.

In this scenario, an offer has clearly been made by Gary, evidenced by his words that he is willing to sell his car for £2,000 and intends to enter a binding agreement. There is no question of this being an invitation to treat. However, the issue is whether the offer is open for Sandeep to accept. There are a number of rules on when an offer comes to an end. For example, it is ended by revocation, by a refusal or by a counter-offer. Sandeep's initial response is to offer £1,500 and this would be treated by the law as a counter-offer, which has the effect of ending the original offer (*Hyde* v *Wrench*). Gary then appears to repeat the offer, by saying that he would accept nothing less than £2,000. It could be argued that because he had already offered to sell to her at this price, he would expect his words to be understood as meaning that the offer was still open. This is quite different to the situation in *Gibson* v *Manchester City Council*, where the council said that it 'may be prepared to sell'.

The rules on acceptance are that it must be unambiguous and must be an agreement to all the terms. Assuming that Gary intends his words as an offer, Sandeep now clearly communicates her acceptance of this offer. This will become a binding contract, regardless of the fact that Gary has sold the car to someone else.

There seems to be no evidence that Gary has revoked his offer. He could have done this through a third party, as in *Dickinson* v *Dodds*, but Gary does not seem to have made any effort to contact Sandeep. It seems likely therefore that the contract will be treated as binding, with a valid offer and a valid acceptance.

ⓔ **8/8 marks awarded.** In order to achieve high marks for problem-solving questions, there must be explanation *and* application. Notice how at each stage of the answer the rules are stated and then applied to the situation involving Gary and Sandeep. It is important in this type of question to use authorities to illustrate the explanation and support the application. But notice that the answer does not explain the rules in detail because there is no time to do this.

Question 11 Breach of contract and damages

Sandeep later agrees to buy a car from Dodgy Motors Ltd, a second-hand car dealer. She agrees a price of £2,500 and the company agrees to deliver the car with a full service and MOT. When the car is delivered, it does not have an MOT certificate. Sandeep accepts the car but has to spend £250 in order to get it through an MOT test. She sues Dodgy Motors Ltd for breach of contract.

(a) Briefly explain the meaning of breach of contract. Assuming that there is a contract between Sandeep and Dodgy Motors discuss whether Dodgy Motors Ltd is in breach of contract. (8 marks)

e The command word ' explain' requires you to give a definition and 'discuss' means that the explanation has to be applied to the facts and some comments made.

(b) Assuming the company is in breach of contract, outline how the court would calculate an award of damages to Sandeep. (8 marks)

e The question asks you to 'outline'. This requires an explanation of the rules on calculating damages, but also some application to this particular situation.

A-grade answer

(a) Whenever a party fails to perform an obligation under a contract, it is said to be in breach of contract. Actual breach is when there is a failure to fulfil an obligation under the contract or to fulfil it to the required standard. Anticipatory breach occurs when one party shows by express words or by implications from its conduct at some time before performance is due that it does not intend to observe its obligations under the contract.

The rights of the injured party depend on the nature of the term broken. A breach of warranty is a breach of a minor term that does not go to the root of the contract and only gives rise to a claim for damages. A breach of a condition is a breach of an important term, giving the right to terminate the agreement and repudiate (cancel) the contract.

It is clear in this scenario that Dodgy Motors is in actual breach, as it has failed to fulfil the contract to the required standard. It was agreed that the car would be delivered having been serviced and with a valid MOT certificate. Sandeep's rights will depend on whether the breach is treated as a breach of warranty or a breach of contract. The law prevents someone using a minor breach of contract as an excuse for cancelling the whole contract. It does seem likely that delivering the car without an MOT would be treated as a breach of warranty because it seems that the car was broadly sound and Sandeep was able to secure an MOT for it. She would not be able to cancel the contract and her remedy would be limited to damages. She would be able to recover the £250 she spent getting the car through the MOT.

ⓔ 7/8 marks awarded. This answer does not refer to any authorities, but it does explain the rules on breach of contract clearly and then applies them to the scenario. It discusses at length whether the breach would be treated as a breach of condition or a breach of warranty, as this is clearly the main point at issue. Time is not wasted on unnecessary elaboration, e.g. by discussing anticipatory breach more fully, because this is not central to the facts in the scenario.

(b) The purpose of damages as stated in *Robinson* v *Harman* is that 'when a party sustains loss by reason of a breach of contract he is, so far as money can do it, to be placed in the same situation with respect to damages as if the contract had been performed'.

There must be a causal link between the breach of contract and the damage suffered, and it is evident here that Dodgy Motors is responsible for the condition of the car.

The courts have to decide how far the losses suffered by the injured party should be recoverable. The principle used is that losses are recoverable if they are reasonably within the contemplation of the parties as a probable result of the breach.

In *Hadley* v *Baxendale* it was stated that damages should only be awarded for losses that could fairly and reasonably be considered to have arisen naturally, in the usual course of things, or those as may be supposed to have been in the contemplation of the parties at the time they made the contract, as the probable result of it. The application of the principle can be illustrated by the case of *Victoria Laundry* v *Newman Industries*.

It seems reasonable to assume that Dodgy Motors would have understood that a failure to deliver a car with a valid MOT would result in expense and that therefore it is liable for this expense.

However, it is the duty of every party claiming damages to mitigate loss. This means that they need to ensure that as far as possible losses are kept to a minimum. The claimant cannot recover for loss that could have been avoided by taking reasonable steps. But they are only expected to do what is reasonable. *In British Westinghouse* v *Underground Electric Railway of London* it was said that a claimant would not be expected to 'take any step which a reasonable and prudent man would not ordinarily take in the course of his business'.

In this case, the loss suffered by Sandeep could have been mitigated by her taking the car back to Dodgy Motors and giving the company the opportunity to get the car through the MOT test. There is nothing in the facts to indicate that Dodgy Motors was incapable of servicing the car properly and preparing it for an MOT test.

ⓔ 8/8 marks awarded. This answer contains a full and detailed explanation of the rules on how damages are assessed and refers to a number of appropriate authorities. It then carefully applies these rules to the scenario.

Knowledge check answers

1 This is the physical element required for criminal liability — literally the 'guilty act'. It is made up of all the parts of the crime except the defendant's mental state. While most crimes require the accused to commit a certain act, this is not always the case, and criminal liability can also arise through a failure to act (an omission) and from a certain type of conduct.

2 Because the victim's injury was no longer an 'operating cause' and the negligence of the doctors constituted another causal chain.

3 That a jury could only decide the defendant had the necessary intention if they believed that at the time of the killing the defendant foresaw death or serious injury as a virtually certain result of his actions.

4 That if during that series of acts the necessary *mens rea* was present, that was sufficient coincidence to justify a conviction.

5 Because the kind of crime to which a real social stigma is attached should usually require proof of *mens rea* especially if it carried a lengthy custodial sentence.

6 That 'immediate' need only mean 'imminent' — the harm need only be apprehended in the immediate future and not the next minute.

7 Definition: 'any hurt or injury calculated to interfere with the health or comfort of the victim', provided it is not 'merely transient or trifling'.

8 Crime and Disorder Act 1998.

9 Because they can be more closely tailored to the needs of the offender, e.g. an anger-management course.

10 Elements include: a curfew requirement, an exclusion requirement, a mental health treatment requirement and an alcohol treatment requirement. There is also a supervision requirement, which puts the offender under the supervision of a probation officer for up to 3 years.

11 Because she was not proximate to the scene of the traffic accident — she heard it but did not actually see it.

12 Judges are reluctant to extend the categories of negligence because this could lead to a large number of cases coming before the courts.

13 Because she had to be compared to an average, competent driver. (Think what the consequences would be for road safety if it was acceptable for learner drivers to drive with a lower standard of competence.)

14 Because the risk of harm was very low and the cricket club had taken sufficient precautions to guard against that risk by erecting a high fence.

15 The three requirements are:
- The doctrine is dependent on the absence of explanation.
- The harm must be of such a kind that it does not ordinarily happen if proper care is taken.
- What caused the accident must be within the exclusive control of the defendant. If the defendant is not in control, the doctrine does not apply.

16 Because it was foreseeable that the claimant could receive burns from dropping the paraffin lamp into the hole.

17 These comprise quantifiable financial losses up to the date of trial and are assessed separately from other awards because the exact amount to be claimed is known at the time of the trial.

18 Pain and suffering, loss of amenity and the injury itself.

19 (a) County Court — fast-track
(b) High Court — multi-track

20 On the basis of the value of the claim and the degree of legal complexity.

21 An offer is an expression of willingness to contract on certain terms, made with the intention that it will become binding on acceptance.

22 An invitation to someone to make an offer.

23 An unqualified and unconditional agreement to all the terms of the offer by words or conduct.

24 It is the idea that each side must promise to give or do something for the other.

25 Social and domestic arrangements.

26 That they are presumed to be legally binding.

27 When a party fails to perform an obligation under a contract.

28 When one party indicates (by words or conduct) at some time before performance is due that he or she does not intend to observe his or her obligations under the contract.

29 To place the injured party in the same situation with respect to damages as if the contract had been performed.

30 Those losses not reasonably in the contemplation of the parties as a possible result of the breach.

31 Doing what is reasonable to keep the losses to a minimum.

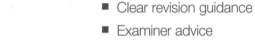